a story

that took a long while being told

and is very difficult to share

Cover design: Bazmi Rizwan Husain

Front cover: Reading the pages of an Urdu diary (Photograph by Neelima Sharma)

Back cover: De-stress; a macramé headrest by Aban Zehra Husain (Photograph by Bazmi Rizwan Husain)

Sara's family tree: Kabir Bazmi Husain

Content formatting: Shama Husain

Page layout, printing and binding: Notion Press

psychlinis

a story

Shama Husain

Notion Press

Old No. 38, New No. 6
McNichols Road, Chetpet
Chennai - 600 031

First Independently Published by author under pen-name Shama Ansari
Re-Published by Notion Press 2018
Copyright © Shama Husain 2018
All Rights Reserved.

ISBN 978-1-64249-673-4

My life has been a tapestry
Of rich and royal hue,
An everlasting vision
Of the ever-changing view.

Carole King

Contents

Author's note

Many years ago I read an Albert Einstein quotation somewhere: 'Reality is merely an illusion, albeit a very persistent one.' The thought is intriguing. To me nothing seems an illusion anymore, everything seems like reality, someone's reality at some point in time. I have dared to think that the reverse seems equally plausible, that an illusion be seen as an ephemeral reality; transient, yet true for that moment. I have come to believe that however unreal it may seem to someone, however bizarre, it is real for someone else in that moment of time; even though this reality may shift in the very next instant.

The writings that follow explore these different realities, short-lived as well as long term, and how different people perceive them. They also explore the multiple realities of someone with manic depression and try to make sense of the apparently unreal world of the mentally and emotionally ill.

I dedicate these writings to my parents. My father would have understood what is written here, just as he understood my need to write and encouraged it; my mother would have this story told gently, tentatively, so no one is hurt. I hope I am able to tell this story with my father's keen insight and in a way that emulates in some measure my mother's remarkably understated tone.

I also dedicate my writings to my maternal uncle, who wrote for a living and painstakingly taught me to read books when I was a young adult. He thought I was beautiful and deeply intelligent and did not hesitate to tell me and others so.

These writings remember a scholar, poet, friend and psychiatrist. From the many books on anxiety he gave me to read, I sometimes wrote down my thoughts.

I am writing this for those of my family who are also close friends, and friends who have come to be like family to me; for the children of our friends and for the friends of our children. I am using their words and the words I have spoken to them. For this I feel privileged and would like to acknowledge each one from the deepest recesses of my heart and mind.

These writings also brought into my life some young people who lent further meaning to my translations of Urdu poetry, gave a new voice to parts of the narrative and made breathing space for some of my breathless lines. In quest of linguistic propriety, a close friend watched out for me and I am immensely grateful for her help and encouragement in a myriad ways.

I specially write for my daughter. She has given me a graphical, three-dimensional understanding of the supposedly two-dimensional bipolar disorder, which seems to have more than two poles. I would have liked to include the graph here and dwell on it. Unfortunately my understanding of the mathematics involved is transient and limited, but it is from her that I have understood that this illness is complex in its multiplicity.

I feel a deep sense of gratefulness to my son for quietly reading all that I have sent his way, sometimes for a long while without comment, so it is easy to forget that he is still reading and listening intently. When I am writing, it feels as though he is standing behind me, reading over my shoulder, and that is a strangely comforting thought.

I owe the fact that I write at all, to my husband, someone who is hard to describe, leave alone emulate. I have aspired to do the former in these writings and the latter in life. He believes I can do anything if I set my mind to it and this belief has taken me a long way in becoming who I am.

I also write for myself. Memories fade and feelings are not rekindled that often. If we don't capture these moments, some of the unshared time gets lost in personal nostalgia.

This is the story of Sara Ibrahim, a woman just turned 60, who has had bipolar disorder, also known as manic depression, for all of her adult life. She tells this story through the writings of her elder son Azad, her own prose and snippets of her own and others' poetry, some bits and pieces of songs, a few pages of her mother's diary, letters she wrote to her children and any other evidence she can find that shows her to be more than the sum total of her illness.

The story has truths taken from various quarters and placed in different settings. Some truths have been deliberately left out, so as to protect people and not cause any intentional hurt. I draw on my own and the collective experiences of many people. The few pages in Urdu were written by my mother. I have taken the liberty to translate and include these with some minor changes to fit my narrative.

Meet Sara

Girl with a sultry complexion

Zaheen aankhein, kitabi chehra,
Woh sanwali ek udaas ladki.
Safed aanchal se tan ko dhanpe,
Mere dareeche mein jhankti hai

Intelligent eyes, an expressive face
That sad girl with a sultry complexion.
In a white shawl wrapped around her,
Through my window she peeps in.

My friend, she and I played together,
She has known me for years together.
Coming with the last rays of the evening,
She graces my house with her presence.
Then with her slender, cool hands
She covers my eyes.
We play the game of guess and tell;
She loses.

She comes into my room, looking
At the beauty and elegance all around.
She opens all parts of my wardrobe,
One by one.
She drapes the ends of my new *saris*
Over her shoulders;

She tries on and assesses my jewellery,
Old and new;
Then she goes near the mirror
And tucks in stray strands of her hair.
She turns around and with a lament in her eyes,
Pulls at my heartstrings.

I say to her, 'Come, sit down,
I will show you the ways of the world,
Where I have wandered
I'll tell you tales of the world.

I will explain new ways to you, teach you new styles.
All these things that you see, about them I will tell you.
All these *saris* are from France, look at the floral work,
The purses are all from Italy, see the matching footwear too.
You see these ice-blue sparkling gems,
These are diamonds, did you know?
And these are not artificial pearls,
They are real, do you concede?

It is true that the importance of things in life is but transient.
Do you know that the perfume in this tiny bottle
Is the most expensive in the world?
I have done all this shopping,
If truth be told it is priceless.
I have looked through thousands of shops,
And only then chose each thing.

But listen, what is this moistness lurking in your eyes?
Come out of your courtyard, see,
This world is very large.
Leave the tight confines of your two low-ceilinged rooms,
Leave also the wet earth and the tree in the corner,
Demolish the weak wall in whose shade you lost everything,
That torn bamboo screen in the verandah,
If possible pull it down.

This is my world, come into it,
It is clean, clear and pleasing to the heart.
There are privileges, there are realities,
Here every colour is blossoming.'

My friend, she and I played together,
She knows what I say.
She smiles in an undertone,
And with a gentleness accepts everything I say.
She says to me, 'Come let us play again,
The game of guess and tell.

You say there are privileges and there are realities in the world.
Why is there an existence of realities?
What is the nature of privileges?
What are the principles of truth?
What is the validity of friendships?

On the brow of privileges are evident my tears,
Did you know?
In the very blood of realities are included my dreams,
Don't you agree?

The efficacy of friendships, my abandonment, my separations,
The principles of truth are simply my long-forgotten stories.
I am the custodian of your dreams,
I give you my memories for safekeeping.
If possible, these things that you have shown me,
Take them away...'

Coming with the last rays of the evening,
She graces my house with her presence.
With the first rays of dawn
She goes her way.
That sad girl with a sultry complexion,
Who has known me for years together.
Who can say, who can tell,
Whether she wins or she loses?

Extract translated from *Meri Saheli* by Zehra Nigah

Impressions

Starry

Starry night

Paint your palette blue and grey

Look out on a summer's day

With eyes that know the

Darkness in my soul.

Don McLean

...and then one day on a warm, sultry afternoon, just before I turned 21, I lost myself in Lutyens' Delhi; not just in its glamour, but in the illusion of reality it created. The monsoon was over and autumn had yet not set in. A storm had passed, or so we thought, and this was the lull before the next one. But it was not really a lull at all, as the winds had begun to pick up already, howling and pushing up small tornadoes of dead leaves by the side of the broad streets, leaving me with a hollow feel in the pit of my stomach.

I went into a large jewellery shop with its glittering, fiery gems set in yellow and white. With only a few *rupees* in my purse, I let the saleslady in the shop try pieces of jewellery on me and I felt like a princess. Perhaps I seemed like the princess of some lost era to the attentive salespersons, with the single diamond in my nose and my long, silken hair brushing the back of my knees. It is hard to tell what they were thinking and harder to guess what I was, as I tried on jewels worth millions of *rupees*.

In this part of Delhi there was a magical place with white buildings surrounding a lush central lawn. Like a concrete snowflake sitting on a blade of grass; with its three concentric circles running parallel in a never ending circular path and radials that came out from the single centre; the diverging rays connected these paths, which never would have met otherwise. To me it seemed it was not mindfully so and the radials just happened to meet these circles on their way out of the sanctum of hundreds of thousands of dreams, on their way to meet the rest of Delhi and the world.

This is Connaught Place, CP as it is called. It was designed by Robert tor Russell, a fact I was oblivious to when I roamed these circles and radials, uninhibited, very alive and in the gayest of abandons, with a song on my lips and glorious music in my heart. Cliched, as a young friend pointed out, but there is no better way to describe a state of being where everything holds meaning and promise, and all senses are alive and alert. CP has been renamed Rajiv Chowk, a fact I wish I did not know. It would have made me very angry when I was young, but now only fills me with a weary disdain. I walked, danced, trudged wearily on, and was dragged through these broad avenues, but was left stranded at the unformed threshold of adulthood.

The shops in Connaught Place were so pretty, nothing like I had seen, nothing like what existed in my little town; yet it was so near my hometown, only two hours by train. Going to Delhi as a child was a treat. It meant days walking around in the Connaught Place and Janpath areas and dusk spent in the central lawn, snacking on biscuits and *namkeen,* or salted snacks, drinking 25 *paise* glasses of iced water from the carts, chatting, playing games. As night fell you had to be careful as men, some young, others not so young, would take cover of darkness and walk close by, brushing against you, reaching out to touch your growing, hurting breasts. That is why you were never supposed to go anywhere by yourself. My younger sister and I never did, yet that did not stop these men from finding us and groping. It did not change anything if we told someone, the protective adult did not really listen, only heard and replied, "But I told you not to go by yourself to that side," and then held our hands so tight, it hurt.

As a child I knew what it was to stand at the exact centre of this *chakra*, this wheel, and set it rolling. I would hold out my hands straight in front of me, cross them over and hold on to my sister's hands, to spin around as little girls often do, everything a blur around me, my two braids flying out behind, my feet moving like a whirling dervish. My sister would cry, "Stop, Sara! Oh please stop!" but I would not, not for a long, long while, till the sound of the whizzing wind in my ears became so very loud, painfully loud. Then I would simply let go of my sister, who was thrown out, a little tearful, very dizzy, sometimes nauseous. I would then bring my arms down by my sides, stand in one place and take a last spin like a stick standing on one end, then fall straight to the ground with my eyes closed. When I opened my eyes and looked around, the white wheel that was CP was spinning about me like a merry-go-round, oh so fast it was difficult to breathe. I was still not sitting on the merry-go-round, I never had, but that was not important anymore; I was making it spin. I had started it going and I was at the hub of this whizzing, whirling world.

This whizzing wheel lost its appeal after a while, but my sister wanted more and so I went along. It did not matter so much to me that she did; I did not need to stay trapped inside this *chakra* any more. My soul had found another escape and could take my mind and heart with it. All I had to do was open my eyes as soon as I fell and look straight up at the sky above me, instead of the buildings around. Look at the blue sky that took on incredible hues I had no words to describe or examples to compare with, although I had been up in an aeroplane already, but that must have been at night; I do remember the lights on inside the cabin and you never turn on lights during the day, I was taught. My spinning head made my spirits spiral and sent them soaring, high above Delhi, straight into that vast, blue expanse with its few puffs of soft, white cloud floating around. I never looked down, as then I might have felt giddy and been afraid of the height I was at, maybe even slightly sick. I knew that if I was able to really let myself go, then I could reach this divine blueness. I could never describe exactly what it felt like. I was glad to be with my sister, happy to have been playing with her, but now I was flying high, elated, euphoric and ecstatic; states I was later told were not normal.

It was incredibly quiet up there, a quietness I would always crave, a quietness I would always cherish, a quietness that was not an intrusive, numbing silence. It would take me tens of years to find it again and then only briefly, rarely. The touch of these wispy, moist clouds did not break the quiet and I could stretch out my hand and touch them. I did not know then that these clouds came together sometimes and could bring down a deluge that would drown the world. It was still many years before one such deluge would fill the fields around my home, as I watched from the normally sunny terrace my father had designed, while he and my twin brother Kamran carried an emaciated, starving, malnourished, dying woman from a flooded field. The woman had hollows for eyes and looked as though rigor mortis had set in even before death came to her. I watched them carry her in from the fields, put her in a *rickshaw* and take her to the Medical College Hospital just to the right of the house. Had I seen this image when my thoughts were flying high, I would have fallen from the sky and hurt myself.

I did fall from the sky one day and the sky came down on me, when my father was carried to the same hospital in much the same way, even though I was not there to see it happen. I was with my younger sister, 130 kilometres away in Delhi. I could not come to terms with it.

My younger sister's name is Mariam. I have an older sister too and we call her *Apia*.

The six of us, *Amma, Abba, Apia,* Mariam, Kamran and I, swathed in sweaters, shawls, coats and mufflers, piled into *rickshaws* to go to the *numaish. Numaish*, which literally means 'on show' in Urdu, was what this magical carnival in our hometown, Aligarh, was called. It was an exhibition, a fair, a fabulous market of handicrafts, with colours and spices, tapestry weaves and silks, bangles and perfumes, toys and water balloons, film songs and lovers, a merry-go-round, a ferris wheel, a circus, and loud sounds with a ring of merriment to them. There were loudspeaker announcements about lost children and special events. Jewellery shops sold intricate pieces and their sparkling gems caught the lights and were set on fire. Barely lit tents beckoned with cauldrons of sickly sweet *halwa* and greasy *paratha* that we were not allowed, and the more refined *seekh kabab* and *naan,* which we were; but best of all were the finger bowls at the end of the meal, with very hot water, just short of scalding your fingers, and an eighth fraction of lime to take out the Dalda *ghee* from your finger nails. I judge restaurants today by how good their finger bowls are!

It was a gala event of enormous proportions for our small town, at the coldest time of the year. The gravel in the broad pathways of the fairground was watered by hose pipes every afternoon so the dust would not rise into people's eyes. Sometimes it would rain or a few tears fall, of young children and broken hearts.

Rickshaw pullers pulled their heavy load on the way back from the fair, stopping to catch a breath at the railway crossing, which stayed closed for long periods, as one eastbound train followed another at that late hour.

There was the circus too, with scary clowns who had red hair, like the cook in that house across the street when I was a little girl. He put henna in his hair and told us stories as he rolled out *rotis,* or unleavened flatbread. The stories were always about our dolls. He said our dolls would come to life when we slept and some of them would do wicked things to us. He was just a silly, old man, not quite so sinister, but we did not know this at the time. One day he did a very wicked thing to my sister Mariam and me; he pushed us into a small, windowless room, a *kothri*, at one end of a brightly sunny courtyard and locked us in. He laughed as he left. It was pitch black in there. I knew where the dolls were sitting, on a shelf in the corner, and the sound started out as tiny little whispers, inside my head, but coming straight from that corner.

The voices did not grow any louder that day and when we were shot out into the blinding sunshine after what seemed like an eternity, we ran, not looking back to see who had let us out, straight across the small street, through the prickly hedge, and into the safety of 7 Shibli Road. I became afraid of orange hair, of hair dyed with henna, of hair dyed any colour. This fear receded into abhorrence then repugnance, and lingered as a distaste forever.

Our new house, Mishkat, was ready when I turned 15, and it was our family's last year in university housing, *Abba* had guided many research theses in the shade of its half built walls and *chhajjas,* awnings, and he was very excited about moving to Mishkat, an excitement I think I did not quite share. One day I got together with a friend a year older, who shared the school *rickshaw* with me. I took my whole collection of beautifully crafted, handmade dolls to her place. We locked ourselves in a room on that sweltering summer's day, turned on the ceiling fan at full speed, and as we smoked through an entire packet of cigarettes that I had stolen from my father's carton, we threw each doll up into the fan and watched it shred into several hundred pieces, spilling out the stuffing; we watched clothes rip, hair fly, tiny gems from beautifully handcrafted jewellery fall everywhere and left the disastrous mess of tiny hands and feet there, to be swept up by the *ayah,* the housemaid. I never turned back to look at the devastation we had caused, never paused to consider that maybe this was a sort of self-induced emotional lobotomy, one of many I would perform in the years to come. I felt no pain, no remorse, no shame, only defeat. I don't know what my friend felt; she is a brilliant scientist now and maybe she has forgotten all about it.

I did save one doll though, given to me by a pastor's wife in faraway Halifax, Nova Scotia, an African-Canadian girl doll. She was *kali gudiya*, black doll to us, very dear to my heart, more than the two *gori gudiyein,* the fair dolls, with rosy cheeks and pink lips, which we had too. As my eye went lazy so did the doll's, but she grew with me and never did anything wicked. She now sits on a mantelpiece at home, where our CDs used to be, a dark chocolate jazz symphony.

I have not been to the *numaish* for a lifetime of years now. Still, I will never forget how joy and fear, good and bad, pretty and ugly sat side by side in this show, just as they sit in our minds. There was a glittering, shimmering main gate that took you to the bright side of the fair, with women and children, families, couples newly married and even groups of school girls in their school uniforms, if it was the early part of the evening. If you wandered afar you would be in a darker, shadier part of the *numaish* that smelt different, unclean. Tent flaps would open and you would see strange things going on inside, sideshows and gaudily painted women sitting with young men who had oily hair puffed in front and wore tight, tubular pants, just like the last Mathematics teacher we had at school. Beyond this dark side of the fair lay the circus tent.

I was always afraid to let go of another's hand in this teeming fair, afraid I would get lost, afraid that no one would hear the announcement of a lost, little girl with two plaits. How could they when there was such loud sound everywhere? There were also these voices sometimes inside my head, louder now since the day I was locked in the *kothri*. They must have been in everyone's head, as I was the same as they, or so I believed. I would strain and listen, and sometimes I could not make out the name of the lost child. It could have been my name I could not hear; that others would not hear either, to come look for me. I get the same feeling today, of being lost at brightly lit airports and train stations and supermarkets, with their undulations of sound.

And then one day I grew up from a skinny, awkward, sometimes quiet, sometimes extroverted child; 'mostly extroverted,' as my *Abba* told everyone; into a person. It was only rarely now that I wanted to bury my head in a pillow and pull the covers high over my head, to stay in bed, afraid to come out. The voices in my head were still there, but I could now implicitly take ownership of them; these voices in my head were from somewhere else, but they were not alien anymore, they belonged to me and did not bother me as much. What I did not know was that in just a few years all this would change and I would grapple with a terrible reality which would change the meaning of the very word for me.

A young mind

I remember, I remember,
The house where I was born,
The little window where the sun
Came peeping in at morn;

Thomas Hood

When I read this poem by Thomas Hood through to the end, I seriously doubted that we could have studied it in Class III. But in Class III, or at the most Class IV, while our school was still in *Papa Miyan's* house, I was given this poem to memorise and recite with actions. I clearly remember the little window through which the sun came peeping in, the roses red and white, the violets and the lily cups, these flowers made of light, the lilacs, the robin, my brother, the laburnum (that I had difficulty pronouncing), the swing, the swallows, and the fever on my brow, which I prosaically acted out by placing the back of my hand on my forehead. I don't remember the rest; maybe they edited it to make it more childlike. *Apia,* my older sister, gave me a red, net frock with a satin lining to wear, which she used to wear for her *kathak* dance recitals. The frock came to my ankles, but I wore it proudly.

I was the child of a university household where everyone studied, everyone read and everyone went to a school of one kind or other. I knew no different, and until much later, thought that every household was the same. It was a protected childhood, but never crowded, and we were allowed plenty of space. *Amma* and *Abba,* our mother and father, were university teachers all their working lives, while continuing to study too. Academics was for them a matter of personal choice; therefore, we too made our own academic and personal choices and they never interfered. Except when *Abba* would try to bribe one or the other of us to become a drama artiste instead of a medical doctor, or an architect instead of a scientist. It was partly in jest. The rule of thumb was that we would go to them if we wanted help or advice, which we almost never did. They did not come to us, to scrutinise or oversee our work, or get into the nitty gritty of our emotional lives. Not until years later, when *Amma* had no choice but to involve herself in every aspect of my life, and I had to allow her to. *Amma* and *Abba* had studied Education and Psychology respectively, but on principle they did not apply this learning to their children. *Abba,* however, had his own peculiar brand of psychology that he applied to us. We were ranked in school and when the reports came there were varying shades of disappointment, depending on each one's rank. So *Abba* started giving each of us money depending on order of rank. If you came first you got one *rupee*, if you came second you got two *rupees*, third, three *rupees* and so on. Once Kamran made out like a bandit because he came 17th in class. *Abba* was not rewarding success; he was addressing perceived failure. It worked; I have never been left with a sense of failure, no matter how unsuccessful I may have been in the many endeavours of my life.

Apia was my parents' first born, born to them when they were both students and were ill-equipped to start a family. Our paternal grandmother, *Ammi Saheba,* stepped in and took over *Apia's* early upbringing. She was an only child for 11 years and has always related to us more as an elder than as a sibling, standing a little outside our tight threesome. Only now, when I have more grey hair than she and we have both been through some life changing experiences, do those 11 years not seem to amount to much any more.

On 2nd October 1957, my twin brother Kamran and I were born, as different as any two human beings could be. Right from infancy we formed a bond that threatened to exclude everyone else, as it would have, but for the nature and structure of our family. We were not to form a duo as there were a large number of cousins at home, plus an aunt and a grandmother, who ensured that we spread our affections thin. The term 'odd' was disallowed. I think of it today, as Kamran and I were both odd, in totally different ways. Even so, we were close to each other, despite being different in our oddities. My quiet, almost autistic twin, who found it difficult to relate to anybody, began to relate to words and numbers instead. He saw numerical patterns everywhere and wrote enticing stories about them. I did not understand him and wanted to pull him out of himself. After every argument he would throw me to the floor and pound the stuffing out of me in sheer frustration, because I was glib while he could not find the words to say what he wanted to. My children were shocked when I told them this, and for a long time I could not explain what brings out violence in us, when the need to inflict hurt finds expression in the gentlest of human beings. *Abba* did not let anyone interfere with him, with their well-meaning advice, although he sometimes said, "*Ama yaar Kamran, tum aadmi ho ya pajama?*" Oh my friend Kamran, are you a man or a pyjama? Sounds such a rebuke but it is not at all; it is the most gentle of reprimands. *Amma* read to us incessantly, so Kamran could create his own world with words and mathematical imagery. And he did. His is a sound and decent world. You can, after all, learn to relate and even excel in relatedness. When we were in our teens he used to say, "Sara, you have to carry your own cross," yet every time, in every crisis, he comes running halfway across the world to carry it for me. And sometimes comes running for no real reason at all.

My earliest memories are staccato, disjointed, but not in the least disturbing. I feel that we first remember something, and when we have this a short time and distance behind us, it becomes a memory. A little later in time and perhaps from a greater distance, we make a memory of this memory, and that stays with us. My earliest memory of a memory dates back to when Kamran and I could not have been much more than two years old. *Ammi Saheba* fell and broke her leg around then. I have a clear recollection of her leg suspended from the ceiling, which I described to someone when I was four. There is no photograph of this and I don't remember anyone talking to us about it.

I was born, or rather we, Kamran and I, were born in a house called Khalil Manzil on Marris Road in Aligarh, and we lived in that house for about four years. There are hardly any photographs from that time, but when I described to *Amma* many years later, the row of large rooms with a verandah running the whole length and a large courtyard adjoining the verandah, she was surprised that I knew the house in such detail. She was even more surprised that I knew there was a hand pump for water in one corner of the courtyard, just outside the kitchen. It was an old house and the kitchen or *bawarchi khana,* the quarters of the cook, was removed from the main house.

When we were little more than two and a half years old, our youngest sister, Mariam, was born, the beauty in the bundle. She grew up to be deeply intelligent, gorgeous to look at, sharply focussed in whatever she did, matter of fact. She brooked no nonsense and never got into trouble, not because she was good all the time, but because she was clever and just stayed out of the way. Watching my own daughter Ghazal through the years, I could see many of Kamran's and Mariam's traits in her.

Mariam was born in King George's Medical College hospital in Lucknow, and when *Amma* came home after a difficult birth, she was carried up the steps in one of the dining chairs, as she could not walk. The tiny baby girl was in her lap. Kamran and I, eagerly circling the chair, were asked politely but firmly to move out of the way. I remember the cocooned baby in *Amma's* lap, protected against the bitter winter's night, the four legs of the chair carrying her, jutting into our faces and the tone of *Abba's* voice, strained with worry for *Amma,* as he asked us not to get in the way.

When Kamran and I were almost four, *Amma* and *Abba* took their four children and set out for Canada on a teaching/study assignment. The majestic ocean liner with its labyrinth of corridors, in which Mariam got lost once because she decided to go in search of dinner on her own, started its journey from Bombay on the 9th of August 1961, amid pouring rain, loud thunder and blinding lightning. The passport says our family arrived in Quebec on the 15th of September, after almost six weeks of sailing. Directly they made their way to 111 London Street in Halifax, Nova Scotia, which was to be our home for the year that followed. Some years ago Kamran took his children to Halifax to look for this house, but it does not exist anymore. Though its picture still lives in my mind; of the house and its surroundings, down to where the light switches were and how I reached them, the kitchen sink where *Amma* bathed us, the dog that chased me in the backyard, the nights sleeping next to *Apia,* the floral curtains in the living room, which had a claret red carpet, the toboggan ride, the snow, the snowman, the wooden, front patio bathed in sunshine...

Then there was the smell of winter as autumn bowed itself out behind a rust and orange curtain, but before the snow came; a freshness mixed with a certain smokiness, as in smoked ham, that made you want to take a deep breath and savour it.

A lady met *Amma* on the bus one day, a reverend's wife, who was very taken with this tiny, academic woman from India travelling by bus with three little children, in a foreign country. She wanted to help, and it came about that she would pick up Kamran and me from our respective nurseries each day and take us home. In the evenings *Apia* would pick us up from there. This lady's family became an integral part of our lives. Without imposing their culture and values on us, they gave us much that we carried back with us, just as they took much from us and made it a part of their lives. It is this lady, our Aunt Catherine, who gave me the African-Canadian doll that I have hugged to myself for half a century, because it spoke to me of inclusion of cultures, a rare privilege.

Speaking only Urdu and being plunged into a totally English speaking world was like jumping into a *vak*, the hole Swedes make in the ice of a frozen lake, to jump into for sport! Kamran never spoke much anyway, but I froze up and became mute for close on four months. I am told I became much kinder to Kamran during that time when I closed myself behind linguistic walls through which much went in, but nothing came out. These walls closed in but did not stifle, were not suffocating, at least I don't remember them to be so; my aural senses were acutely alive as was the processing of what filtered through. I was an intense child and this intensity became inwardly directed. In prolonged, dead silence my mind deciphered the English language and stored it away. As a result, I awoke from a nap four months into our lives in Canada, in Aunt Catherine's home, and decided to speak. Only Nanna, the grandmother, was there and sitting across her in a spot of sunlight at their dining table, I related my entire four-year-old life to her without pausing to breathe, in more or less correct English. Many of *Amma* and *Abba's* Indian friends came to see this phenomenon, but I would not perform. "*Hum Urdu logon se* English *mein baat nahin karte,*" I don't speak in English to Urdu people, was my standard response. I have been a balanced bilingual since, leaning a little towards English now.

My childhood was school and home, with little variation. There were friends at school, whose faces are a coagulated mass in the early years, and I cannot decipher individual bonds until much later. At home there was our house and a neighbourhood. Many people lived with us at home, including older cousins who came to study at the university there, propelled by my parents towards higher education, rather than a quick job. It was cramped quarters and there was no concept of private space, except for *Amma* and *Abba's* room, which too was always open for one or the other of us to crawl into their large bed in the dead of night, traumatised by a bad dream. We knew no different and it did not bother us. At home and in the neighbourhood I can pinpoint individuals with whom I had specific relations from very early on in life. One of these was my paternal aunt who had come to live with my parents. Pivotal in managing this large household, she took on the upbringing of the many children who lived there and the parental lines merged.

Nanphu to us, she became a vital link between my children and my parents, as they grew up and my parents were no more.

We were only allowed free movement on our own street and no further, and we had to be home at sundown. The thrill was to sneak out without *Amma* and *Abba* finding out. Nights out, or sleepovers as they are known today, were rare occasions of great excitement and always involved a midnight feast, which was food stolen from the dinner table and eaten cold on the dot of midnight! With no television, computer or internet, there was only the Grundig spool player almost exclusively used by our parents, the radio to be shared by the many who lived with us and later an HMV Calypso record player. And our own imaginations. When growing up, I used to often tell Abba that I was bored. He invariably replied that it was a good thing to be bored. This reply used to irritate me no end. Now as an adult I can see its wisdom. Boredom is bland and devoid of stimulation, so it neither takes you up nor brings you down, but leaves you in a state of suspension that is quite therapeutic. In small doses though. It is, by no means, an ideal mental state to be in for long periods of time; that would turn you into a vegetable. But it is alleviating after mental turmoil and angst.

The school was our local, coeducational, convent school, where children of university teachers, as well as everyone else, studied. Every year the nuns would threaten to make it a girls' school, but that could not be, as where would the boys study then? So to this day, it continues to take in boys; and the nuns, these gentle creatures of god, are made of sterner stuff than we think. They have the wherewithal to handle a coeducational environment with hormones running amok at puberty. I attended this school with my brother and sister, with my friend Adil and his brothers, some near and far cousins, other children of this tight university community and some from the city beyond the railway lines, the *shahar*. It was an ordinary kind of school that did not follow any particular pedagogy. I was an ordinary kind of school pupil, thin as a stick, with two, long braids hanging on either side of my face and large spectacles with soda bottle glasses in them, which covered half my face. It was here, behind the newly built school hall that I smoked my first cigarette while two of my friends kept watch.

Adil and I both agree that it was a great school. I can't remember what we learnt here, but we must have learnt something. I was a studious child and recall doing many homework assignments, for others too, especially in Physics and especially for Adil and his friend, who came on cycles to collect their ill-gotten goods. They invariably ran into *Abba,* who was quite forbidding at his jovial best to young boys cheating on their homework. I only remember one other interaction, actually encounter, with Adil. Our class X was going up the stairs of the new block under construction, with sand and cement mounds piled on the landings. Adil reached the top of the stairs and with his foot, pushed some sand down. As his luck would have it, I had just climbed the first step and it all fell on me. I didn't say anything, but when I reached the top I picked up a fistful of sand and rubbed it into his face, teeth and ears. Adil was mortified, though he tells me that he was secretly quite pleased, and everyone around was shocked, as this was more physical contact than we were allowed!

In the years just before high school we studied Mathematics entirely on our own as there was no Maths teacher; the puffy haired and tubular trousered gentleman having left. Therefore, we were not allowed to take Maths in high school: my first brush with academic fate that I had to reckon with for all my years of higher education. Biology was my bane, but I studied it much in my undergraduate years as I could not study Mathematics. I found out then that, 'Horsica atlantica' is not the biological name for seahorse but the figment of someone's ingenious imagination back in school! I hated Chemistry with a passion but kept studying it for reasons unknown, right up to MSc, as a kind of self inflicted torture. When I pitch this schooling against what I have done in life, I can only say that the school let us learn the way we would have learnt best, independently. I have learnt best that which has not been taught to me at all.

7 Shibli Road was our home where we came of age. This low-cost university housing was where we hàd our first lessons in life. There was a front lawn and a back lawn and in the back lawn was a *gulmohar* tree that shed orange red flowers on the green grass below. I remember shimmying out from between the bars of our bedroom window when we were actually supposed to be taking a nap, to spend many sunny afternoons there, winter or summer. That is where I learnt to be bored. In the front lawn *Amma* planted rose bushes, gerbera and a frangipani tree on top of a rockery that housed many cacti, some of them quite deadly. I remember rubbing dough into my fingertips to remove the needle-like thorns. Near the rose bushes and next to the front patio was a Chinese jade plant, a succulent with fat, deliciously sour leaves. For my first fast, called *roza kushai*, during *ramzaan,* I had decided that rose petals and Chinese jade leaves do not count as food; as also the nutty gynoecium of marigold flowers stolen from the neighbour's yard. Mariam and I made ourselves quite sick on these and were not quite ready for the *nariyal ki barfi,* the coconut sweet, made specially for us to break our fast with *iftaar* at sundown. The back lawn was surrounded by a red and white lantana hedge and we used the florets to make necklaces for our dolls. The front had a red hibiscus hedge, known to us as 'shoe flower'. As our school rickshaw passed this hedge on the way out, we grabbed a few flowers to give our shoes a quick rub, or there would be hell to pay with our dear nuns. Inside there was a courtyard where we slept on summer nights. Along one wall there were, a papaya tree and a *goolar* tree, a variety of the fig. No one wanted to sleep under the *goolar* tree as it dropped its fruit, splat on the ground, or on the faces of whoever slept under it, and little worms came out with the ooze!

With our next door neighbour, a very serious gentleman whose daughters were our best friends, I had my first roaring argument about the questionable existence of god, much to *Abba's* chagrin, which he let me know in no uncertain terms. I was eight then. For some time after, I actually had a brief tryst with Islam, fasting almost the entire month of *ramzaan* and reading the *namaaz* five times a day. Not too long after, the incomprehensible greys of Islam began to give way to the vibrant vermillion of Hinduism as I entered my teens. I was less interested in the philosophy, more in the traditions, rituals and colour, studded with the dramatic gems of Indian cinema. Playing *holi* was a problem, as people came too close and the colours turned to muck. I would lock myself in the bathroom when university students came to play *holi* with *Abba.* Once *Abba* hid outside the bathroom door and when I came out he hugged me closely and rubbed his cheek against mine. All hell broke loose and I threw the mother of all tantrums. You see, we were a family who shook hands, and this was a transgression that was not acceptable. When I cooled down and the offending colour had been showered off, *Abba* talked to me for a long time, again something he rarely did. The next year Mariam and I were sent to my friend's house to stay the night, to usher in *holi,* and in the hope that I would overcome some of my fears. Late at night they built a magnificent bonfire in the central square of the Railway Officers' Quarters, to burn the demoness *Holika.* Each of us was given a sugarcane pole at one end of which was tied a bunch of red gram branches, akin to chickpeas, with the bean pods intact. With the long pole as an extending arm, we singed the branches, then popped open the pods to eat the *hola,* the roasted, red gram beans inside. I have not eaten *hola* since and the only thing I can compare the taste to is Swiss *Marroni*, the roasted chestnuts I buy on the streets of Zurich. I don't remember sleeping that night, but I do remember being woken up to don white clothes and take a dip in the *houda,* at least that is what I remember it being called, a small stone tank built in the courtyard just outside the kitchen, normally used for storing water. A multitude of flowers had been soaking in the *houda* for 24 hours or more, and their colour and scent had infused the water. The water was biting cold but the perfume was heady, intoxicating; our white clothes were coloured the bronze, orange, red, pink of a floribunda rose.

Recently I had *saris* made for my large family of sisters, cousins, a niece and an aunt. I worked with two wonderful designers and a weaver from Tamil Nadu. They took the bright orange warp of one of *Amma's* old Kanjivaram silk *sari* borders and crossed it with wefts of different colours: black, purple, green, blue, olive green, to produce many shades of this bronze, orange, red, pink colour that I cannot forget.

It was a very special visit, but I still did not like *holi.* As I grew out of this phase, I kept only the colours, to merge with the colours of South India, and my personal belief bordered on a kind of Sufistic atheism, where all was inside me. I stopped looking to religion altogether. *Amma* and *Abba* never ever discussed religion with us, except once, when *Abba* said that if he had to pick a religion, he would pick Buddhism. Late in *Amma's* life and from some of her writings, I know with certainty that she derived strength only from within herself. She has been the most significant role model in my life, even as I am my father's child in temperament and Kamran is hers.

Christianity was never a religion, it was a storyland, a musical; as we read our picture bible, dressed up branches of the thorny *babool* as a Christmas tree, dressed ourselves in old sheets to play out nativity and vied with each other to be the beautiful Mary, sang Christmas carols, and ate *kampat, a* hard, fruity candy, caramel toffee and Britannia cake, for want of anything better. The church never entered the picture. Although we were in a Catholic convent, the school chapel was out of bounds and it never intruded upon our school lives. Our Father Who Art In Heaven was sung alongside *Hum Honge Kamiyaab Ek Din,* We Shall Overcome One Day, and we were taught Moral Science instead of The Story of Our Lord. Christmas Eve would find us at the house of our family ophthalmologist, a large and hearty lady with a booming voice, who was a spinster; except that our petite *Amma* always insisted on calling her a bachelor. The house was decked for Christmas and there was a Father Christmas with presents. Once *Mamoon Saheb,* my maternal uncle, was Father Christmas, and this portly gentleman with a pillow stuck over his belly, who was oddly familiar, said to me, most seriously, *"Ek chhoti si chidiya ne mujhe bataya hai ke tum angootha choosti ho,"* a little bird has told me that you suck your thumb. I was mortified and had to go into hiding with my thumb sucking, especially from birds, as my presents next year were in jeopardy. In one half of our host's house there lived a Swiss lady who was married to a very close friend of *Amma* and *Abba.* This Christmas party was for their children. As I recall, everyone else there was Muslim, some devout.

Several people worked for us in different capacities. One was *Barey Miyan*; *barey* means big, but here it stands for old, and *miyan* is used to address a man or a boy with affection and respect. He was stone deaf, but able to talk in a way in which the last of the sentence would be stretched out to a wheee... as he could not hear himself and did not know where to stop. He was our *bawarchi* or cook. In the summer evenings he cooked outside in the *sahan, aangan* or courtyard, but it was best on winter nights when we could take our plates into the cosy kitchen and sit around his *angeethi,* the iron bucket of coal fire used as a stove, and he doled out puffed up *rotis* from which you had to release the air carefully, so they didn't give you a steam burn. The food kept warm in covered *pateelis or* saucepans, had a taste that I am trying to emulate for my children as they develop their own recipes.

Food was mainly meats — *kofte ka saalan* or meatball curry, *shaami kababs* or beef patties, *pasanda* or thin steak strips marinated with spices, fried in a *karhai,* wok, or baked in the Wee Baby Belling. It was always beef never chicken, as the latter was too expensive, and mutton was only for that very special occasion. Vegetables were cooked with meat — *aloo gosht* or meat and potatoes, *paalak gosht* or meat with spinach, meat with beetroot, meat with turnip, meat with okra. I have tried cooking all these since and developed a taste for them, although back then, we liked our meats straight or with potatoes. There was always a *daal,* pulses or lentils, cooked like a soup, and our favourite was *kali daal,* brown whole lentils, because it was *Apia's* favourite and cooked in large quantities every time she was home from college. In the dimly lit, warm kitchen we could talk whatever nonsense we wanted as *Barey Miyan* could not hear; we did talk nonsense, acted silly and mouthed obscenities that we dared not utter if we could be heard.

One night *Barey Miyan* finished his work in the kitchen, cleaned up and retired to his small room outside the courtyard wall. When he did not come in at his customary hour the next morning and several hours passed, *Abba* and I went to see. The door was locked on the inside, but the small, barred window was open and we looked in. He was lying there on his back, absolutely still, with not a muscle moving. Not realising that it will do no good, *Abba* and I shouted and banged on the door. Then we picked up a handful of pebbles and aimed these at him. Nothing worked and we went back to the house. *Abba* looked quite worried as he and *Amma* had a serious, hushed conversation. Just then *Barey Miyan* walked in, his appearance dishevelled from too much sleep, and said, *"Der ho gayeeeee,"* I got late. Abba almost hugged him and said, "Hum to samjhe tum gaye," we thought you were gone. That is the day I first heard the word *inteqal*, death. By inference my mind interpreted it as a state where you went to sleep and didn't wake up, and were permanently gone. Half a century later this still is pretty much what I know it to be and have difficulty wrapping my mind around its permanence.

Bhikku, a young lad about our age, used to do odd jobs around the house and his mother Ramshree used to clean for us. When *Amma* asked Kamran to go to the shops, he would immediately pass the chore onto Bhikku and upon his return would adjust the price of things in the accounts to *Amma,* so that the change matched the balance from expenses. *Amma* was very particular about accounts and Bhikku could not do even the most basic arithmetic. Kamran's philosophy was that accounts should add up, no matter what happened in the actual exchanges. It certainly pleased *Amma,* though I have sometimes wondered about Kamran helping Bhikku fudge accounts! Many years later I was listening to *Amma* reminisce and was very surprised to learn that she knew all along.

On summer nights beds were laid out in the *sahan,* with pristine, white sheets and white mosquito nets hung from bamboo poles at each end. Mariam and I shared a bed even when we were quite big. Some nights when there was no power and so nothing to do inside the house, Mariam and I would lie across our bed and dangle our feet, which did not reach the ground. Looking up at the billion stars in the sky above, we sang Hindi film songs from these little booklets sold outside cinema theatres, which we read by the light of a kerosene oil lamp. We had not seen any of the films, but had heard all the songs on All India Radio. One or the other cousin would oblige and get us the song books that cost just a few *paise.* I don't know where the stars have disappeared to now, though I kept the little booklets for a long time.

Every evening the *anda, dabalroti, makkhan wala,* the egg, bread and butter man, came on his bicycle, his big, tin box rattling on his carrier. From the top of a slab of ice inside this box, he produced 25 gram *tikias or* sticks of butter. This is a really small amount of butter and sometimes *Amma* would buy just one *tikia* to go around for all of us. But there was always enough. I do not recall a single instance when we felt there was not enough food for everyone. A hot favourite was *matri biskut,* large rounds of puffed up, crisp, hard bread infused with *elaichi,* cardamom and eaten with lashings of *baalai* or *malai,* the thick cream skimmed off the top of milk, and Kissan Mixed Fruit Jam. Everyone who grew up in Aligarh ate *matri biskut* and you can imagine Adil's absolute delight on discovering the same taste in Kardemumma Skorpor in Sweden, years and years later. He lathers it with butter and dunks it in his tea, so the butter floats on top of the tea.

Ammi Saheba, our paternal grandmother, lived with us at 7 Shibli Road. To take care of her there was a nondescript lady by the name Anwar Jahan. Her resplendent moustache made her the butt of many jokes, at which she took great umbrage. *Ammi Saheba* was operated upon for goitre when she was quite old and the surgeon was related to *Abba.* After the surgery *Ammi Saheba* became very weak; her doctor and

Abba decided to put her on a diet of beer every day so she would gain some weight, and told her it was *Angrezi joshanda,* English medicine. Chilled beer was kept in the fridge for her and Anwar Jahan was the unlikely bartender deputed to pour her a glass every afternoon. This went on for several weeks until we decided to disillusion Anwar Jahan. I, being the outspoken one, was asked to do the deed, which I did. "Anwar Jahan, *ye dawa nahin hai ye to sharaab hai aur sharaab peena ghalat baat hai,"* Anwar Jahan, this is not medicine, this is alcohol, and it is wrong to drink alcohol. Poor Anwar Jahan threw up her hands and saying, *"Hai Allah!"* Oh my God, she went running to *Ammi Saheba. Ammi Saheba* did not say anything to anyone, but from that day on she did not touch the brew. Later on she told *Abba* that she was too old to try new things.

I loved sitting close to her, as she had the softest skin and smelt of sandalwood soap, my favourite. She taught us Urdu from *Das Din Mein Urdu,* Urdu in Ten Days, by Hayatullah Ansari. Mariam actually mastered Urdu in ten days while Kamran and I took much longer. She was a very strict teacher and shoddy work just did not pass muster. She taught us the *kalma,* the stated consent to being Muslim, and then she taught us the *namaaz* and the *roza.* From her we got stories from the Bible and the Quran as well as from history. From Anwar Jahan we got wild fairy tales of demons and princesses, seemingly never ending stories that could go on for weeks. I must confess I liked the latter more.

I was 12 when *Ammi Saheba* passed away after prolonged illness. It was the first time in my life, perhaps the only time, that I saw *Amma* cry, behind the open door of her wardrobe. *Ammi Saheba* was like a mother to her, even when her own mother was still alive and she was not married to *Abba.* The closeness had only grown and she felt orphaned by this loss. It was my first encounter with death, with loss that I actually felt and mourned with a 12-year-old's mind. The mourning was, of course, tempered by what I thought was the right decorum in such an instance. So in the weeks that followed when everyone went to see the film *Waqt*, including Kamran and Mariam, I chose to stay at home. Not because I wanted to be a martyr or did not want to see the film, a rare treat, but because that film, any film, or for that matter any activity, would interfere with my thoughts of *Ammi Saheba* and I felt that would not be right. These were not depressing thoughts or bad thoughts; neither were they angry thoughts or fearful thoughts; they were good thoughts and carried with them the touch, feel, smell and picture of a person who I would never see again. So my mind made a picture of her that was not only visual, but aural and sensory too, with full knowledge of what it was doing. I used to curl up tight in bed and consciously and methodically go through the sound of *Ammi Saheba's* voice, the feel of her hair and *mulmul dupatta,* the muslin scarf she covered her head with, the touch of her withered fingers on my skin, the strength in her hands as she pulled and braided my hair, the deep lines on her face; a face very like *Abba's,* except *Abba* never got the time to develop these lines. Even at that age I used to worry that just as the person had irrevocably gone away, so would the clarity of these thoughts. I was mistaken. I neither forgot all the sensory perceptions of *Ammi Saheba* that I had accumulated in my mind, nor did I forget to think about them after she died, so I could ensure for myself the memory of a memory. But these memories did begin to fade after some time, or I should say I began to let them go. Today I have to look back to find them; sometimes I do.

When everyone came back from the cinema, Mariam told me the story of the film over several days; she is a wizard at this and could describe the minutest detail of sight and sound. I wore *Amma's* white Leela lace sari with the *pallu* pinned at the shoulder and trailing to the ground, and sang and danced to *'aage bhi jaane na tu, peechhe bhi jaane na tu,'* you don't know what lies ahead, you don't know what has gone by. The day Shashi Kapoor died, Adil and I watched *Waqt;* I saw the film for the first time and it was like watching a dream spun by my younger sister.

Some years later I entered a different kind of reality called 'college.' My college years are hazy in my mind. I do remember playing *Raag Yaman*

Kalyaan on the sitar I had borrowed from a maternal great-uncle, *Nana Miyan*. At some point I had discovered the discotheque and Adil built me a set of strobe lights, which fortunately never worked. I recall studying overnight for several exams, when studying for several days prior to that did not work, smoking cigarettes stolen from *Abba's* silver cigarette case and later buying my own; as well as smoking *ganja*, weed, or grass as we called it then, if the opportunity presented itself; buying quarter litre bottles of whiskey, gin or rum when finances permitted (once someone brought *Abba* an imperial gallon of Johnny Walker Black Label and our life was made; we just siphoned off some, but committed the worst crime by mixing in water, and thus, our misdemeanour was found out), writing poetry and a 27 page letter, waking up early to stay in bed half awake for an extra hour, doubting everyone and everything, and having explosive arguments that sent the other person around the bend, while I kept my cool; on occasion *Abba* had to be called to intervene, as when I verbally pushed a cousin so much, he started hitting his head against the wall while I just stood by and watched. There were histrionics in everything, onstage or off, high drama and rebellion. When I think back it feels as though my thoughts were changeable like quicksilver, hard to hold on to, continuously shifting patterns. In quieter moments it frightened me, but there were few quiet moments in this rollercoaster ride that was my youth.

Past the first year of college, when I was 17, there came a long gap for some reason, a long, unscheduled holiday with nothing to do. *Abba* brought me a set of forms he had received in his department. These were for a camp in the US called 'Encampment for Citizenship,' not US citizenship but good citizenship. The forms asked for small essays in answer to questions that would highlight your understanding of good citizenship and give reasons as to why they should invite you. Didn't seem insurmountable. *Abba* liked me to write, but never read anything I wrote. *Amma* did, but she immediately started correcting what I wrote, so I didn't like to give her stuff to read. The form was simple enough. I completed it in no time and had *Abba's chaprasi* or peon post it for me at the university post office. Quite quickly I got a reply, a fat packet of pictures and information. They had chosen 20 participants from 12 countries, and I was one of them. I could not believe my luck!

The very next day I was dispatched by train with Kamran to get my visa. The visa officer was an affable, middle-aged man who asked me a lot of questions about my family and seemed interested in the fact that *Apia* was in the US, a green card holder. This interview was in a room and the officer very politely showed me to the door, asking me to wait outside. Almost immediately a lady followed with my passport, inside which was a white sheet of paper that said something like, 'Unless otherwise proven it is our statutory presumption that you are an intending immigrant.' At first I could not understand what that meant. When Kamran and I deciphered it, I was crushed with disappointment.

Back home by train, to find Abba pacing up and down the verandah in agitation, rubbing his palms together as he was wont to do under stress. In between inaudible mutterings to himself he asked me questions about my interview. I sat perfectly still, not daring to move. Suddenly he stopped in his tracks, deliberately turned around to face me and in his calmest voice said in Urdu, *"Sara, agar tumhe kabhi bhi Amreeka jana hai to tum is waqt kisi bhi surat ye visa haasil kar lo,"* Sara if you ever want to go to America, then somehow or the other you should get this visa now. How was I to do that? He said that was something for me to figure out.

For some weeks after, I was possessed. What to write, whom to write to? I dragged Kamran to Delhi again, to the USIS. They would be able to give me names and addresses: of the US ambassador to India, of the Indian ambassador to the US, of officials in the US consulate, of foreign service officers in India. Armed with this crucial information I came back home. Day and night merged into a continuous cycle as I wrote in longhand on ruled paper. I have no recollection of what I wrote, except that one of the letters was 27 pages long. I wrote in a passionate frenzy and do remember the feeling of voicing my anger against injustice and discrimination. As each letter was completed I sent it off with the *chaprasi*. Then the semester began and I calmed down, though I was acutely aware that the encampment happened and I was not there.

After some months passed there was a call from the US Consulate asking that I come with my passport in connection with the visa I had applied for. My heart sank. This could not bode well, as the duration for which I had applied for the visa had already passed. What could they possibly want of me now? So with Kamran in tow, I went back to Delhi and was directed to a different room in the consulate. The room had a large desk which was fully covered with sheets of paper, neatly arranged. I could see that some were copies of the various letters I had written. Paired with these were typewritten memos and quickly skimming these, I caught the words, 'grant visa.' When I looked up, there sat a thin, mean looking man behind the desk, with a clipped goatee, short in stature, but large in the menacing look he gave me. He pointed to all the letters on his desk and said in a reedy voice, "Do you think it is your birthright to be granted a US visa?" My reply, vague in my mind, just seems an illusion now and the person was even more put out. He wordlessly held out his hand for my passport and stamped the visa.

Recently my doctor wanted to know what I was like as a child and as a teenager. She wanted to trace evidence of depression in my early years. Such a crucial question hung upon the characteristics of my early years that it was something I did not wish to opine on myself. So I asked several of my family. From amongst them I got three interesting responses: Kamran said he does not remember anything odd as he too comes from the same bipolar strain; *Apia* said I have always been very intense and quite volatile, but not depressed; and Mariam felt I was moody, wanting to be on my own; she specially remembers that when everyone played cards, I would not join in and would prefer to sit it out on the sidelines. No one recalls my being depressed or having a depressive episode.

Was my reality so very different from my peers? In this idyllic setting there are some dark images that cast their shadows. This is, I suppose, true for most childhoods and lives of young adults. These negative experiences through my youth were never allowed to be traumatic and so, did not sit deep in my psyche. In spite of my mental impairment, or perhaps because of it, I was able to leave them behind me and with time have become totally indifferent to them. Telling those stories now would involve divulging confidences. There is, thus, the story of Rosaleen, which I never wrote. As was the demand of our culture and the times, I could not tell my parents everything, though *Amma* instinctively knew all through the years, knew of the slow corrosion of my self-esteem, and she protected me. Nor could I tell my siblings, cousins or friends, who approach an understanding from their own minds, from a reality that is very different from mine. I felt I would become less in their eyes, a tragedy far worse than what I was experiencing. It is perhaps because of this that I have never submitted to any kind of psychological counselling that has required me to talk about myself. After *Abba* died and it was established that I had a different mind, this seems to have been a tacit understanding with my family and all the various psychiatrists who have treated me; that I will not be counselled. Though many have counselled nonetheless, as did *Amma,* that there is little reason to persist in analysing things that you cannot change; there is reason to rationalise and let them go. I have taken that as permission to be my own counsellor.

Ammi Saheba and Anwar Jahan told us stories, a mixture of reality and fantasy. *Amma* and *Nanphu* told my children, Azad, Ghazal and Rumi stories, also a mixture of fantasy and reality. Rumi was five years old when Amma died, Ghazal was about to enter her teens and Azad was already a sensitive, mature teenager. Ghazal hugged to herself *Amma Nani's* fantasy tales, like *akak bakak darwaza khol do,* open the door *akak bakak,* in which a pair of goat kids are eaten up by a wolf and the mum goat comes and slits open the wolf's stomach and frees her babies; quite gory! *Amma* also read tales to Azad and Ghazal from Akbar and Birbal, and Mullah Nasruddin. Rumi was too young for these tales and I could never reproduce the fantasy stories for him. He got it from Harry Potter, The Hobbit and Lord of the Rings.

My stories started with Rumi. We made ourselves a little book on *chaar line ki copy,* a four line notebook, where I would write bits of my story, and Rumi and I drew or painted the scene; yes, with my abysmal drawing skills! The stories went something like this: …and in the corner is the gulmohar tree with its orange, crimson flowers, the tiny, green leaves that are such fun to strip off the stalk with the pointy finger and thumb, and a rough, knobbly trunk that is so good for scratching our backs. I am afraid of climbing trees but Kamran and Mariam are not; sometimes I go up too, but only to the first branch. …*Apia* is 11 years older than Kamran and me, and she is a very serious person; she is studying to become a doctor and sits on a reed mat and reads and writes all day, all the while eating puffed rice and roasted gram out of a biscuit tin. … *Amma* is a teacher and very strict, and there are many, many rules for us; but that does not stop us from non-stop playing. There is so much to make believe and pretend, so many stories to tell and to listen to, so many songs to sing, so many secrets to keep, fights to fight and tears to cry, and there is so little time. …Abba is always in a hurry and rushes about singing rum pum pum tunelessly. It probably sounds to him like the Beethoven or Mozart he listens to on the old Grundig spool player. To us it sounds all the same, but so does the real thing. The only time he is still, is when he takes his shoes out from under the bed and sits cross legged on the floor and polishes them to a high shine so you can see your face in them. It is like meditation for him. We would rather use the shoe flower.

With Ghazal and Azad my stories took on more serious and mature overtones, talking about life and death, loving without reserve, smoking and drinking, and so forth. Ghazal says, in her Grade 10, I told her class how *Abba* came upon us smoking weed in *Amma's* dressing room! If she says so, I must have, though I cannot imagine in what context.

Very early on, Azad started writing his own stories. When he found me writing all the time, with or without Rumi, he asked me what I was writing. I told him I was writing a story. "Your story, *Ammi?*" and I said, "No, that you write." So he wrote me four chapters of my story that have transformed my narrative into a story of my life.

Penned by Azad

Sara's Family

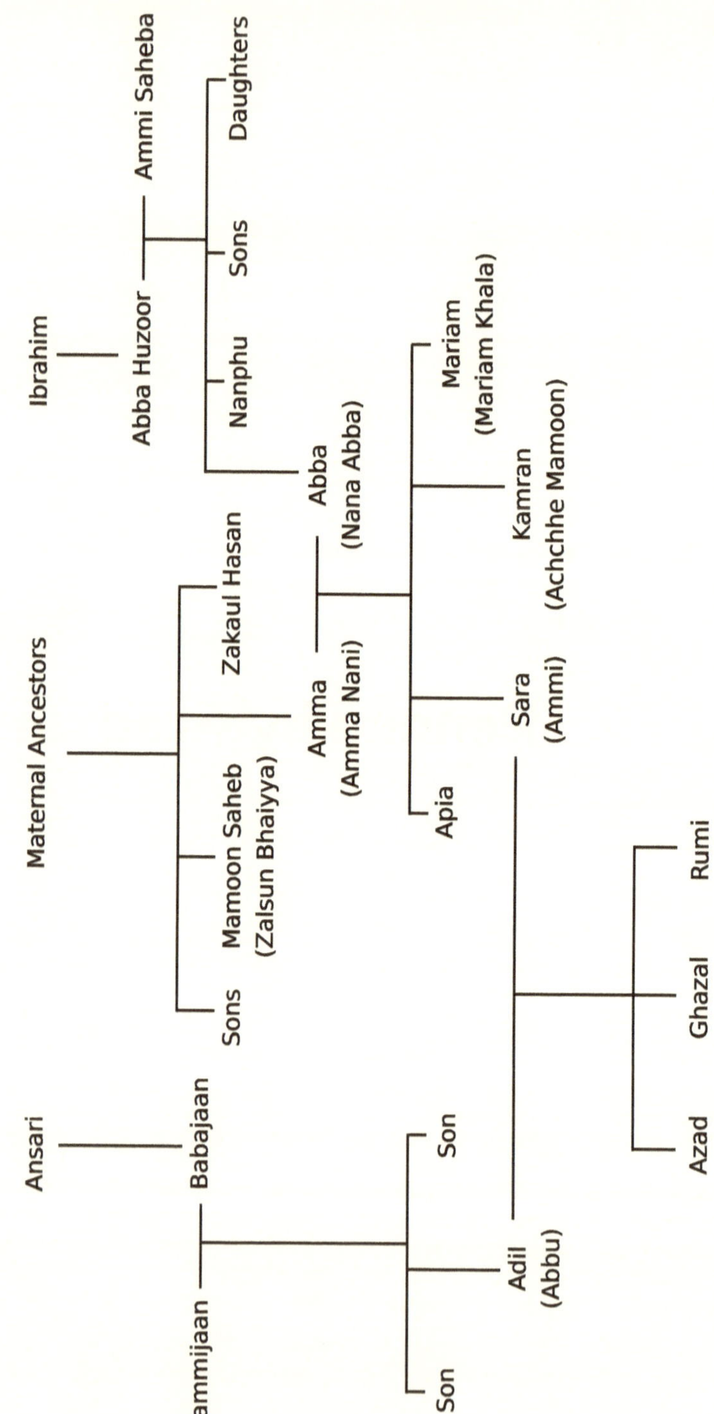

Chapter the first

I, Azad Ansari, sit on a small, wooden jetty, from where no boat has sailed for a long while now. Somewhere halfway up the eastern coast of Sweden lies a small village where an avid sailor owns a beautiful, sun drenched summer home, which my parents leased some years back. The backyard of the house rolls southwards and tumbles into the mouth of a river where it gently joins the Baltic Sea. My parents are not sailors, but a small boat remains tethered to the jetty, to honour the spirit of a friend who fights the battles of life and celebrates each victory by taking to the sea. It is not his boat, it is just a boat in not very good condition, but it serves as a metaphor of a revered philosophy of life. There are many things my mother, *Ammi,* does not understand, cannot understand, which she is afraid of. Then she finds a parallel. The little boat stands for freedom from this fear and for courage, a courage *Ammi* did not always have but respected in others and made a part of her life in some way. Slowly she could lay claim to this strength and courage as she found her own little boat. That learning is an inherent part of my upbringing, a part of my very being; an unquestioned legacy passed on to me, to my brother Rumi, who is the youngest and needs it most, and to our sister Ghazal,

Al Di Meola plays from the house, Orange and Blue, like bunches of nasturtiums that sit in a slightly cracked, cobalt china tea mug in the dining room. Strains of the music ride on the balmy, gentle breeze as it turns nippy and the winds pick up as the sun unsuccessfully attempts to set. The sounds come down to keep rhythm with the calm waters, now turning a little choppy against their will. As I unscrew the cap off my claret and golden Sheaffer fountain pen, handed down from my grandmother, my thoughts unsettle, beginning to race ahead of themselves. What is it that I am attempting to write? Is it the story of my *Ammi's* life or someone's long-forgotten memories? Or is it just a story so deeply rooted in reality that it seems reality itself? It does not matter, as somewhere in it lie truth and learning that stand testimony to my life. Just as the fountain pen does, though I know full well that much of this will be written on the computer; or even the blue, folded aerogrammes my mother wrote in an even longhand, each line taking on a deeper meaning than the hundreds she wrote in email.

Ammi, whose name is Sara Ibrahim, was a child born in free India, brought up when India's freedom was well established. This freedom ran in her veins, never to be compromised and never taken for granted; reiterated in her every action but never yelled out, never even uttered. It was not the abrasive kind of freedom that liberates when it shocks and hurts. It was a rooted freedom that took wing without causing so much as a stir. It was an amazing kind of freedom, so solid yet so effervescent, that I often wondered if it was ever really there. Or was it created in my mind so I would always be free? It was not an aloofness but a very deep involvement lay at its foundation, binding even as it set free.

Ammi is the twin sister of *Achchhe Mamoon*, which translates literally to 'good uncle.' His name is Kamran and he is the closest to *Ammi* of all her siblings. He lives in Delhi and comes very often to visit. The anticipation of his visit brings a song to my mother's lips and a smile to my father's. *Abbu* would hunt out his best bottles of wine and the few slivers of exotic cheeses he kept hidden in the nooks of our rather large fridge. One of us would be sent off on our cycle to buy fried, salty *moong daal* and cheeselings, heavenly centimetre squares of puffed cheese crackers that crackle between your teeth and leave a dry, salty, bitter taste that defies description and has few equivalents on this earth. Also a bottle of Lime Juice Cordial so the youngest would have something to toast with; I was never the youngest. The rest would go to make tall glasses of gin and lime, the first drink *Ammi* ever had without knowing that it was spiked with gin; she had to quickly sit down at a bus stop and thought she had a heat stroke.

Whoever went on that cycle, usually Ghazal, escaped the frenzied preparations in the house, which the other two were subjected to. *Ammi* is a taskmaster and a perfectionist to boot and all of us avoided being around her at such a time. Only Ghazal always eluded *Ammi* as she had a knack for not being around the wrong place at the wrong time; Rumi and I were not so wily and we were given much to do. The spare outside room, the *bahar ka kamra,* that normally served as my parents' study, was turned inside out to become a guest room and informal living room that would resound with friends' laughter and poetry and music later in the day. Two mattresses laid on the ground, one on top of the other, were to be *Achchhe Mamoon's* bed at night and a lounger until his bedtime. A crisp, white *chaader* or bed sheet, was stretched over the mattresses and tucked in on all four sides. *Ammi* believed that making a bed is an art and *Abbu* gave in, tongue-in-cheek, specially when he could set his slaves, us, to do it for him. The sheet had to be stretched just so and all four sides had to be even. Not a wrinkle or a twist was acceptable as the sides were tucked in. That sheet, so malleable in our mother's hands, completely defied us and does to this day as I struggle to make my bed; which, I must confess, is not very often made since it left my *Ammi's* keen scrutiny.

A *Punjabi Phulkari* bedspread, the long satin stitch embroidery worn slightly thin from frequent 'occasional' use, but still vibrant with life and colour, would cover the clean *chaader* on the lounge bed, with a bounty of cushions and *gau takias* or bolsters that brought instant spring to the rather sombre room. Books and papers, unanswered letters, unpaid bills, half-filled application forms, newspaper cuttings, magazines, the computer and *Ammi's* old typewriter were all pushed far back against the wall at one end of the big study table. Their place was taken by instruments to fill the room with rich sounds of music. Pride of place went to the old Grundig spool tape recorder that promised Faiz Ahmad Faiz and Begum Akhtar in the original; then came the record player *Ammi* had bought with her first scholarship grant and on which she listened to Bob Dylan and Carole King, her introduction to western music; vying with these was the small, blue, bubble of a cassette recorder that had taped Jazbi *Saheb* and Zehra *Khala* in my grandparents' home and on which *Ammi* had taped October Cherries singing Jesus Christ Superstar in high school; in later years my father's prized CD player joined these, teaching us Jazz and the Blues, Rock and Country music from small, boxy bookshelf Bose speakers.

For *Ammi* no music has ever sounded as these did. Maybe these sounds so filled her being that there is no room for new ones; or maybe the new sounds go and fuse with the old. I cannot say. Our house is always filled with music, but it is always *Abbu's* music, or mine, or Ghazal's and Rumi's. I am always taken by surprise when *Ammi* puts on music of her own accord, and especially if she chooses an album we do not associate with her. I asked her once and she said, *"Sunte sunte aadat si ho gai hai, aur ab achchha lagne laga hai."* I have heard it so often, it has become a habit and now I quite like it. There were many things that were like this for her. She never fought things that were not a part of her, yet she never sacrificed her person to them either. And at some point the two became indistinguishable.

Chapter the second

It was the 23rd of November in an undefined year of my life. The clock showed 7:30 in the morning, in Västerås, Sweden. I had to leave in a few minutes to see what their out-of-the-box architect/artist had built: a hotel at the bottom of Lake Mälaren and another hotel on a treetop, which fell down recently and had to be restored. His next proposal is a structure on the moon. I cannot help but marvel at this courage to dream, to have such strong conviction in one's own thinking.

I looked out of an upstairs window of Thuregatan 5, which sits on a rocky hillock. The sky was laden with clouds and dawn was just a promise in the southeastern sky, the long, inky night carrying a hopeful tone of grey tinged with a slight orange hue. Maybe the orange hue was just my hopeful imagination. It had been raining for several days now, if you can call it rain. Usually it's a wet mist that envelops you with a cold that seems to seep in. The last two days though, it had rained steadily at an even tempo. It lasted an entire 48 hours and was what my mother described once as a *tip tipua,* the deliberate, drop by drop, heavy rain that seems to last forever, unwavering in its intrusion; which poorer folk in India, living in makeshift houses and huts, so dread. An old man in her mother's village said, *"Jor ki barish huay to phasal ko labh jaroor pahunchat hai, par i tip tipua se bahut dar laagat hai. Oo ki awaj kan mein ghusay jaat hai aur oo chhappar pharh kar hamaar jhupariya mein aavat rahe."* If it rains hard it will certainly benefit the crops. But this drip drip is very frightening. Its sound just keeps going into the ear and it seems to want to tear the thatch and come into the hut.

After weeks of fiendish, unbreathable hotness, when monsoon hits UP in Northern India, the skies darken with heavy clouds, layers and layers of them, snuffing out the scorching sun like a candle wick in molten wax. The lightning streaks across, splitting the skies with its cold, knife edge blade, releasing torrents of water held within. The parched earth almost rises up on the heat fumes to meet the quenching waters in a steamy union of dry and wet, hot and cool. Soon water begins to fill every pore of mind and matter, and if you are young and uninhibited, you run out in minimal clothing to let the water lash your bare skin until it wrinkles up, and your lips turn blue over chattering teeth. It is a fabulous sensation!

The changing seasons of Uttar Pradesh were *Ammi's* world until bigger changes than these began to define it. Our *Amma Nani*, her mother, and our *Nana Abba*, her father, both came from a small village, Pahitia, near Ghazipur, their homes separated by just a hedge into two distinct worlds, yet inseparable in many ways. I have often mused over the philosophy of life that brought and placed these two lives together until tradition and culture found it unacceptable that they be bound so. When *Ammi* spoke about her parents we would bristle with protest at the unfairness of their situation, annoyed that she did not feel more strongly against it. I mistook her silence for tacit acquiescence of an unjust and backward thinking, which I know she did not subscribe to, and it bothered me. Many things bothered me about *Ammi*, until I began to see similar traits in us, my brother and sister and me; even in *Abbu*. And very slowly I began to understand the larger pattern we were all a part of, a pattern that *Ammi* had certainly not designed or engineered, but a pattern that she and *Abbu* have woven into the rich, warm tapestry that is our life. A tapestry that has space for each one's very different thinking, perhaps at odds with one other at times, but not with the larger pattern.

Nana Abba was one of several children of a big *zamindar* family, a landlord farmer who owned a large and flourishing estate. Lands of this estate were not leased out to farmers in the conventional sense; instead, farmers worked the lands of the estate in return for a generous stipend. In addition, their families lived on the estate and were provided for by it. So, in a sense this was not really *zamindari*. *Zamindari* was later abolished as a malpractice that exploited the lesser farmer. Yet, if anyone looked into the structure and functioning of this small community, they would have been impressed by the benevolence, the consideration, the mutual give and take and the feeling of privilege that were its hallmark. There was harmony and contentment born of genuine caring. However, there were still differences and inequities, whether explicit or implicit.

My great-grandfather, *Nana Abba's* father, *Abba Huzoor*, which literally translates to 'Father Sir,' the patriarch of this small community, was a giant who could eclipse any public or personal gathering simply by his presence. He was a freedom fighter, was educated at King's College, London, had done his time in jail for his country, had impeccable manners, was widely read and well educated, was a lawyer by profession, and was inexorably bound by the traditions of his family and culture. The estate was run on his principles with an iron hand and no one dared take issue with him on any score whatsoever. No one needed to, or wanted to. His family was well provided for and the small community was provided for almost as his own family.

Abba Huzoor's household was run solely on his lawyer's salary and the household needs were defined accordingly. No excesses were allowed and no luxuries denied. The estate was strictly a nonprofit organisation and not a *paisa* generated came into the house for any personal profit. *Ammi Saheba*, 'Mum Lady,' his lovely wife, was ultimately responsible for this and her word was law in the house and in the financial management of the estate. The produce was brought in and sorted, to be sent to the market and distributed amongst the families of the estate, including their own. It was an equitable distribution according to each family's needs and anything left over was sent across to the poorer families in the village. Any income generated from the estate was put back into the estate: to pay the farmers' salaries, for better equipment, or repairs to the main *haveli*, as their house was known, for the maintenance of the other houses where the farmer families lived and for everyone's healthcare and medical expenses. A trust was formed to provide scholarships to the boys of each family and a pension to farmer families who had no able-bodied member to work on the lands. For educating *Abba Huzoor's* own boys a part of the considerable inheritance was equally divided and held by the same trust.

"What of the girls in this family, and of the larger community?" we asked *Ammi*. With his enlightened and progressive outlook, did her grandfather not think that he should make provision for the girls' schooling as well? *Abba Huzoor* had several daughters, one being our *Nanphu, Ammi's* paternal aunt. *Ammi* always went a little quiet when this question was asked of her and never fully answered it. She would only say that all the girls of this estate were well educated, even if they were not formally schooled. We knew that her mother, our *Amma Nani*, who came from a farmer family that lived on the estate and was supported by it, had had a well rounded education at home, as had *Nanphu* in the main house. Given the times when not very many girls were allowed the privilege of any education at all, we felt satisfied with this answer.

Nana Abba, home every summer on holiday from college, fell passionately in love with *Amma Nani,* then a slim, demure farmer's daughter in her *mulmul ka leheriya dupatta,* the muslin shawl she had dyed in diagonal rainbow stripes; which later *Ammi* wore and is now kept away for Ghazal. *Amma Nani* would come to his mother for Urdu lessons every afternoon. *Nana Abba* started hovering around with his cup of tea, listening to her recite poems she had composed and even contributing to her lessons. Then one day *Abba Huzoor* discovered that his son was walking this girl home and he flew into a silent rage which only *Ammi Saheba* was privy to. Notwithstanding his great socialist principles, he found this probable alliance totally unacceptable and brought this to the notice of his wife, without really having the backbone to say he would not allow it. Ironically, this was the same person who had adopted *Nanphu* and brooked no discrimination against her. He continued his indirect diatribe against *Amma Nani* and her parents, who did not know anything and would have had no say in the matter even if they did. Then he began to hurl slanted innuendoes at his son. *Ammi Saheba* unflinchingly absorbed everything, displaying a rare moral courage in her silent resolve. He was, after all, her lord and master, and the lord and master of the estate. Meanwhile the Urdu lessons continued and every summer *Nana Abba* grew bolder with his affections, though he still did not cross his father's path. Over time the arguments grew louder and came out of the bedroom.

We did not know until recently that *Amma Nani's* marriage to *Nana Abba* was supported only by his mother *Ammi Saheba,* who was *Amma Nani's* teacher, mentor and strong ally. She did not let the family compromise their liberal values and socialistic principles just because one of their own sons had become involved with the girl of a family of lesser means, automatically deemed of a lower social status. It is all very well to think objectively for others when the truth does not affect you directly, she maintained, but it is a whole other matter to uphold this truth when you are involved in it personally. She was a strong lady and knew she had the reins of the estate in her hands and her finger on her husband's pulse. No one stood in her way when she overruled *Abba Huzoor's* spurious objections of social incompatibility and brought *Amma Nani* home as her *bahu,* her son's bride, with all the grace and class with which she herself had come to the house. She took *Amma Nani's* further education in her own capable hands so she could privately sit for her BA examination. When the newlyweds moved to Aligarh, *Amma Nani* would enrol in the university there to do her BEd. Later she and *Nana Abba* went to London where she was able to do her Master's while *Nana Abba* worked on his PhD. When I learnt to read Urdu my reward was *Amma Nani's* framed poem, *Azad Zahan*, The Free Intellect. *Ammi* said she had named me Azad in the hope that I would grow up to be as free as *Amma Nani* was, free in mind and spirit, unfettered by her lack of station or of early formal schooling.

Nana Abba died before any of us was born, but there is substantial evidence of his scholarship and learning kept away in an old cabin trunk from one of their ship voyages, which is one of *Ammi's* prized treasure troves and sits under my loft bed at Woodsong, *Ammi's* architectural masterpiece in Bangalore. *Ammi* gave me his big, heavy textbook on Abnormal Psychology when I took up the study of Psychology in graduate school. This well thumbed, slightly worn, green, hardbound tome has been a lexicon of thoughts, emotions and actions that has helped me understand and redefine normalcy.

Chapter the third

One of my very close friends recently got married and *Ammi* stitched her a traditional *gharara*, the flowing, rustling pants gathered at each knee to look like a long, divided skirt, worn by Muslim women in North India for their weddings or other celebratory occasions. In Firangi Mahal, Lucknow, which is *Abbu*'s ancestral home, some ladies, including his mother, our *Mammijan*, wore it for everyday use. They would go about the business of household chores, resplendent in the flowing robe, gathered from the back and draped over their left arm. This gave way to more modern clothing with time, which they would camouflage from their elders inside the controversial *burqa,* the robe and veil of *purdah,* as they stealthily went to college to get a modern education; that is the one good use of *burqa* I have found.

The *gharara* is a dress as difficult to describe as it is to pronounce, because it uses a rather French, guttural 'r' for the 'gh'. *Ammi* always laughs at our attempts to say, 'gh'. "Oh, you *firangis*, you foreigners!" *Ammi* laughed. "Remember, Rosaleen! Ghosaleen! Ghazala!" Suddenly she stopped and then said softly, "How would you remember? We never told you."

She still laughed and laughed, a little apologetically now, until tears ran from her eyes, and the laughter gave way to a fit of coughing. *Ammi* is the only person I know who laughs with such abandon, and then cries so much while laughing that she ends up with sinusitis. She says *Amma Nani* was the same.

Rumi noticed, and once said to me, that every time *Ammi* mentions Rosaleen's name she gets somewhat pensive afterwards, thoughtful. Not unhappy, just thoughtful, as though whatever she was thinking of was far behind in time and place. Her eyes seem to go inwards and far away, as though her sight was finding an escape from some deep recess in the back of the eye socket, to look at things no one else could see.

What is it that she saw in the quiet of her mind that she never spoke of? Were these disquieting thoughts that never found voice? Or was it that whatever had to be said had already been said and there was no need to speak of it any more? Sometimes I caught *Abbu* looking at her when she was like that, half with concern, but the other half of his expression always said, "She is all right." Our *Abbu* has enormous confidence in *Ammi*, something we feel she gives herself little credit for, always stepping back a little to hide in his shadow.

Ammi looks somewhat like her mother, from the photographs we have seen of *Amma Nani* when she was young. *Nana Abba* was an avid portrait photographer and *Amma Nani* was a willing subject. We have seen pictures of her wearing every expression possible, taken with a Minolta camera that had somewhere lost its capability to fully focus its lens, like that of a clouded cataract eye. *Nana Abba* would lean backwards and forwards until the picture was in focus, then click. He simply refused to buy a new camera or allow one to be presented to him. He had turned an unused bathroom in the front of the house into his own, private dark room where he would disappear for hours, behind a 'do not disturb' sign. Later on, when *Ammi* and *Achchhe Mamoon* showed interest in photography they were sometimes allowed in to sit quietly at one side, in the red glow of the solitary lamp, and watch him; or occasionally hang up the finished prints. He would then emerge rather shyly with the photographs. Each one of those portraits placed on black card paper, held down with silver corners, and wrapped in tracing paper, is saved in the same cabin trunk that has *Amma Nani's* literary works and packets of old letters. They are some of the most amazing photographs I have ever seen. *Abbu's* very modern SLR digital camera just about manages the same photograph, but those old pictures have a rare quality hard to mimic or pin down. There was something alive in every line and curve, every hue; soft and alive, as though each portrait of *Amma Nani* was *Nana Abba's* own creation, the tones and shades pressed into a canvas with his own fingers.

There are many pictures of *Amma Nani's* eyes, and *Ammi's* eyes are the same shape and colour, just deeper set, like *Nana Abba's* eyes. When *Ammi* is thoughtful, her eyes look a lot like *Nana Abba's* eyes, deep and warm in their sockets as though hugging a secret world to which only they had the key. I have often wondered what his eyes were really like, as whoever took his pictures did not have the same flair for photography, nor the same passion for his features as he had for *Amma Nani's.* Yet you can see the deep seriousness in them, with just a twinkle always hovering at the corners, like it does in my *Ammi's* eyes, taking the edge off serious thoughts and a sombre mood.

Nanphu, *Ammi's* paternal aunt is *Nana Abba's doodh shariki bahan,* a sister who shared his mother's milk. When *Nana Abba* was born to *Ammi Saheba;* a woman in the village lost her life during childbirth, leaving behind a tiny, weak newborn girl. *Ammi Saheba* took her in and nursed her alongside *Nana Abba.* The child's father was in no position to look after her, and *Ammi Saheba* and *Abba Huzoor* legally adopted her. She had the status and position of *Nana Abba's* younger sister, although she was just a few weeks younger than him, and developed a lasting bond with him that is hard to describe.

Nanphu is an acronym of *Nani* and *Phuphi,* great-aunt, a name created for her by *Ammi,* so we would understand the very complex system of naming our relations. Although she is not related to *Amma Nani* directly, she is bound to her as her *guinya,* her *saheli*, her friend, her staunch ally. It is very hard to describe who a *guinya* is, as she is more than a sister or a friend. For those who understand spoken Hindustani, a *saheli* comes close to describing the same sentiment, but not quite. And there is no equivalent for the male gender. So unless one has witnessed it from close quarters, it is hard to translate this relationship.

Nanphu, whose name is Tahera Ibrahim, was Tahera *guinya* to *Amma Nani*, and *Amma Nani* was *guinya baaji* to her, her closest friend and older sister. A sister by marriage but a sister nonetheless, and their friendship dates back to a time when thoughts of marriage could not have occurred to either; except when their dolls were married. Their homes were separated by a hedge that inadvertently separated two social classes in contradiction to the equitable social system being attempted by their elders. This hedge did not stand a chance; *Nanphu* hacked a hole in it when she was just five, because she could not resist the aroma of *besan ki roti* or chickpea flatbread being roasted in a coal *angeethi*, just the other side of it. *Amma Nani's* mother would take out a hot *roti* from the glowing embers and place a generous dollop of freshly churned white butter on it. Then everyone would watch in amusement as the little girl made canals in the butter and bit off the *roti* before the butter ran off. This hole in the hedge only grew bigger. More than just the lure of the *besan ki roti* brought *Nana Abba* through the hedge too, for many years to come. Then one day, a neat doorway was cut into the hedge and decorated with an arch made of fresh jasmine flowers. Eight *kahaars,* or palanquin bearers, picked up *Amma Nani's doli,* her palanquin, and took the bride wrapped in red and gold to the main house. *Nanphu* rode in the *doli* with her new sister and held her hand tight as *Amma Nani* could not help but cry. It was a relationship of two sisters, of two friends who had sealed their bond by some ancient rite, of a mother and daughter although they were almost the same age. Much of what I have learnt about *Amma Nani* and also about *Ammi* and the rest of their family, comes from *Nanphu*.

Chapter the fourth

Nanphu talked without stopping, from the moment I arrived, until I left. It was so quiet in the house that I could hear every whisper, every sigh, each breath she drew and all the silent movements she made. I could almost feel her tears pricking the corners of her eyes. Not once did she touch me, or put her arms around me, as she was wont to do every time we had a serious conversation. This time she knew that just the sound of her voice and the words she was speaking, were touching most deeply, touching my soul as nothing ever had.

"Your mother was very young when she came to us that summer, young, strangely beautiful, frail and raw in her emotions, but oh so strong in her mind. She and her twin brother, got off the train; Kamran, your *Achchhe Mamoon* protectively shielding her from *coolies* carrying luggage and people shoving and pushing. She was not ready for what was to happen to her in the very near future. None of us was ready for it.

Sara was wearing an ordinary cotton *shalwar*, the wide pants worn in North India by young women and old, and in her case almost always white. The straight lines of her *qameez*, the fitted shirt that held her legs together at the knees in the fashion of a bygone era, accentuated her thinness and her height. The white, georgette *dupatta*, the long scarf her mother had edged in exquisitely crocheted lace, kept slipping off her thin shoulders and getting in her way, and she appeared slightly annoyed by it. She kept a stronghold on the white vanity case, browned with age to a dirty yellow. Containing all her mother's jewellery, it was brought to me for safekeeping. Her eyes were large and luminous, like her mother's, with a sadness and an intelligence that should have been at odds sharing such a small space, but were not. She looked around for us, her eyes crowded with emotion, which seemed to suck them back into their sockets, making them deep set like her father's; they almost seemed small. I am glad, Azad, that you have written about these eyes."

"How did you know I have written about *Ammi* and her parents' eyes?" I asked, surprised. I had not shown my narrative to anyone, and most people did not even know that I was writing one.

"I just know," she murmured and I wondered what else she knew; what brought about such confident insight and selflessness, such indisputable feeling and love. I began to see how fortunate I was in the people around me, and how little I took the time to acknowledge it.

Nanphu wanted to describe my young *Ammi* to me in great detail, worried that I might miss something. Nor did she want to get too quickly to the part I had come here to hear about her. I was curious, even anxious, but in no great hurry as I already knew some parts of it from *Abbu* and had been forewarned by *Ammi* that *Nanphu* would take her time. *Nanphu* had a way with words; it was magical when she spoke of *Ammi* and *Amma Nani;* I liked the sound of her gentle, caressing voice that had time and again stilled many storms in my mind. This was familiar ground, only this time she was the one who was going to stir up a large part of the storm. I wondered vaguely how she would manage to still it at the same time, but my faith in her was such that I just gave in to the tone of her voice.

Very softly, so I had to strain to hear, she continued, "Her long, dark brown hair, almost black, but not quite, was plaited low on her back and the braid swung as she moved, touching the back of her knees. Wisps of hair and some long strands too, had escaped from her braid; they brushed her cheek and bothered her left eye. Maybe that's why her left eye fluttered. Do you know what they said when I was growing up? *Pharke aankh dahini, ma miley ya bahini; pharke aankh bayin, beeran miley ya sayin.* If your right eye flutters, you will meet your mother or a sister. If your left eye flutters, you will meet your brother or a lover. Yes, maybe her left eye did flutter.

Adil was a young man, about her age, who came with me to help at the station, as the train stopped in Lucknow for just a few minutes. Sara and Kamran were travelling with their own and their parents' lives crammed into a large number of boxes and trunks and holdalls kept in the luggage car of the train, and these had to be unloaded quickly before the train moved off. I asked him to rush with Kamran to the luggage car. He turned around midway to look in our direction, it strikes me now that he must have wanted to come back to where we stood, to reach out and move the errant strands of hair away from Sara's troubled face and tuck them behind her ears. Although they had known each other since they were children, this was their first meeting after many years and the look spoke volumes; only we were not listening."

At that point, almost without my realising it, *Nanphu* got up to make tea.

Mammijan, *Abbu's* mother, who is *Nanphu's* friend from college and shares the house with her, had left us alone all this while, but she came out of her room when she heard the sound of cups and saucers and crossed me in the verandah to go into the kitchen. As she passed me she pressed my shoulder with her hand; that small touch confirmed a thousand bonds and forged twice as many, with *Ammi* and the three of us, Ammi's children. Voices from the kitchen swirled and mixed with the hum and click of the fan. I could hear them talk, as the two friends made tea together the way they had done so many times before. No matter your preference, in their house you drank Lipton Green Label, unless you were *Abbu,* who was the only one allowed his milky, sugary fare, the Green Label mixed with Brooke Bond Red Label, brewed for a good ten minutes to make it strong, almost bitter. I later discovered that the Green Label was actually Lipton Darjeeling Tea, which came in a green packet, hence, its *takhallus*, its pen name, Green Label. A teaspoon of long leaves per cup, but none for the pot, went into a preheated china teapot; water just on the boil was poured in and then the pot covered with a soft, embroidered tea cosy for exactly four minutes, by when its contents turned into a golden liquid to warm your heart.

I slid down deeper into the folding lounge chair, taking the seat cushion with me, and hunched my shoulders in a kind of moody expectation, even dread. I did not know whether I wanted it over with quickly, or whether it was alright with me to let *Nanphu* take it at her own pace. In any case, I did not have much say in the matter and *Nanphu* did not look like she wanted to get all out of breath talking to me. I heard the creak of the tea trolley. In design school, for my first graded project, I had designed and built *Nanphu* and *Mammijan* this tea trolley from some old pieces of teak and rosewood I had found among odd pieces of old furniture and doors someone had thrown out. They have proudly presented tea on it to countless visitors who graced their cosy verandah, praising it to a station far above its humble, and now rather wobbly and creaky, appearance. I made a mental note to tighten the bolts in it before leaving the next day. The old ladies' relationship with their carpenter never remained cordial, nor lasted long enough for them to get him to do these small jobs.

Mammijan wheeled out the trolley, with all the tea things on it and a blue and white ceramic bowl of *daal moth*, the intensely spicy, very hot, crunchy snack from Agra that burns your mouth with divine heat. The hot tea in turn burns you again, causing an exquisite pain that you wonder why you inflict on yourself. The *daal moth* is specially for me, though sometimes *Nanphu* pops a few flakes into her mouth. Otherwise the ladies eat perfect rounds of Marie Biscuits, thin and pale and quite tasteless with this tea, but which rise to great heights when dunked in *Abbu's* stronger, sweeter cup. Not to beat the *matri biskut* though. The rest of his cup he would carefully pour into his saucer and slurp appreciatively. *Nanphu* and *Mammijan* would never consider dipping biscuit in their tea, nor would they allow us this liberty with the deep gold liquid in their cups.

For some time now I had been accorded the privilege of pouring tea, an honour bestowed on me like repeated knighthood. It has to be done just so. Each cup individually warmed with hot water, the water swirled around and poured out into an empty jug kept for the purpose. Half a teaspoon of sugar is added to each cup before the tea is poured in. It is now that I begin to understand why *Ammi* is the way she is, as I picture the triad of women, first *Amma Nani*, then *Nanphu,* and last but not least, *Mammijan;* after *Ammi* married *Abbu;* who influenced her. The three were perfectionists and so is *Ammi*, even with mundane and repetitive tasks that acquire a new meaning around them. In anyone else it would seem quite exhausting and somewhat ridiculous to be doing ordinary things so exactly, each time, all the time. It would leave no scope for the extraordinary matters of life; but not for the three. For them life itself, at its most basic level, is an extraordinary gift to be savoured slowly and deliberately, with all its nuances and subtleties and flavours. Living life is not a tiring matter and when you do tire on occasion, you rest. Once your spirit is quiet you live to the full again.

For as long as I can remember, when I took the tea cosy off the teapot, I put my right hand inside it, and pressed it to my heart with my left. It was a salutation, an appreciation for the honour of pouring tea. Or, now I think about it, was it something more basic; just the warmth of the tea cosy that I wanted close to my heart, as it reflected the warmth of these two ladies who were so critically important to my mother and me? I remember holding the tea cosy very close and tight in that darkening afternoon and forgetting all about the tea, until the tea cosy was gently pried loose from my hands and replaced by a warm cup. *Mammijan* smiled with her head to one side and said, "The tea was getting cold, *merey bachche,"* my child.

Nanphu was by now, quite tired of narrating her story in such minute detail. However, it was not a story she could make very concise or unemotional, and however hard I might try, I cannot narrate it the way she did, or in the way she rambled, digging up memories and anecdotes. I, therefore, paraphrase the parts she had intended for me. It was the summer of 1978, around mid-August. Her brother, *Ammi's* father, barely 56, had had a massive heart attack some weeks earlier, as he drove out of their home to go to a departmental meeting. After a brief struggle in the hospital, he died. *Ammi* was with her younger sister Mariam *Khala,* in Delhi, at the time; a cousin brought them to the railway station and the two sisters travelled to Aligarh in stunned silence that penetrated each others thoughts, but without solace. *Nana Abba* was larger than life and many people's worlds were shattered by his passing, one of the most broken being *Nanphu* herself. It had been almost 30 years to the day when she left her parental home as a young woman with the newlywed *Amma Nani* and *Nana Abba,* who had brought her with them to Aligarh and encouraged her to pursue progressive learning. Although she had since married, raised a family of her own, had her own home and a teaching job, her emotional attachment to her *Bhai* and *Bhabhi,* her brother and sister-in-law, bordered on filial dependence and she felt as though she had lost her father a third time over.

Then there was *Amma Nani,* who could not conceive of a life without *Nana Abba* and had to muster all her reserves of strength to make herself wake up every morning to the void in her soul. Everyone marvelled at her unfailing courage in the days, months and years that followed, as she took charge of her life and the lives of her children, especially *Ammi's.*

No one looked towards *Ammi,* no one knew just how broken she was, in a manner totally different from everyone else. *Ammi* herself did not know. She was fiercely independent and people around her knew only what she wanted them to. It had always been so and people expected her to act in a certain way, in keeping with her strong personality. In the wake of this tragedy she was there, talking to people, accepting condolences of her peers and elders, offering words of comfort to those who could not bear the loss and had broken down. Many commented that she had her father's character and we know now that there was truth in this. Over time it became apparent that this most assertive independence was born of factors far more complex than a simple question of character. The very characteristics of her mind and emotions that gave her this fiery temperament and limitless passion would cause her to break into little pieces. As it did her father many years ago, when she was only five years old.

Ammi's Mamoon Saheb, her maternal uncle, a thorough gentleman and the senior correspondent of a leftist newspaper, came to stay with his sister, *Amma Nani,* soon after *Nana Abba* died. He was keen that the family move to Delhi temporarily and come to live with him in Jawaharlal Nehru University (JNU). That seemed a possibility. Both *Ammi* and *Amma Nani* idolised him. If our people had the tradition of a godfather, then he would be *Ammi's.* He was her mentor when she was a young adult and he maintained that she had a rare spark of intelligence that was indeed special. Oddly, *Ammi* was the one not too keen to go, though she did not overtly resist. Nonetheless, they made preparations to lock up the house for a few weeks. *Ammi* and *Achchhe Mamoon* had come to *Nanphu* in Lucknow to bring her all of their parents' precious possessions, which included a vast number of books, *Amma Nani's* handwritten manuscripts and her few pieces of jewellery, *Nana Abba's* photographs, camera and printing equipment, as well as some property and bank documents; this was so the family could travel light if they decided to move and their possessions would be safe.

That move did happen, sooner than expected, but not to her *Mamoon Saheb's* home. It was to the psychiatric ward of a large government hospital.

By now *Nanphu* was sobbing bitterly. She said she had helped bring up *Ammi* when she was a child and could feel *Amma Nani's* pain as her own. Controlling her sobs and wiping her tears on a small handkerchief ill-equipped to soak up such a flood, she started again. There had not been much rain that year and they had to bear the sweltering heat of August. The first strangeness that *Nanphu* noticed was when *Ammi* began to dress warmly in the evenings. Her fingertips turned icy cold and she would turn the fan off. Her infrequent expressions of grief gave way to a certain moodiness and sometimes she would talk a lot, her words tripping over each other and most often not making any sense. She stopped crying, but you could tell that she was in terrible pain. There was a day when she cowered in the corner of her room, pointed to an empty chair and with screaming fear in her eyes, whispered over and over again, "Tell him to go away. He is lying, they are all lying." On other days she would be in reasonable dialogue with some other nonexistent person sitting in another chair. She started sleeping less and would feel rested with just a couple of hours in bed. Crack of dawn would find her quite calm, but no one could really reach her anymore. It had been just a week since she had got off that train, so much in control of her faculties. It was difficult to come to terms with this transformation and almost impossible to contemplate a course of action.

Mammijan was married into the Ansari family of Lucknow's Firangi Mahal, though she left home with her husband far back in time and now only visited. *Babajaan, Abbu's* father, an officer of the Indian Civil Service, had just been posted to Lucknow, and they lived in Dilkusha Colony near the Dilkusha Gardens. The family name passed to their sons, and from there to us. *Mammijan* was a close friend of *Nanphu;* and they cared for each other deeply. They shared good times and bad, and almost by habit, called on each other if something went wrong. When matters became such that *Nanphu* could not understand what was going on and was becoming increasingly afraid for *Ammi's* wellbeing, she called *Mammijan* and the two ladies were in quiet conversation late into the night. They talked of other things too from their shared past. From inside they could see *Ammi* sitting in the verandah bundled in a *razai* or quilt, smoking cigarettes non-stop. *Mammijan* suggested that *Nanphu* contact *Amma Nani* immediately, which she did. *Ammi's Mamoon Saheb* came to get *Ammi* the very next day. Many years later, after *Abbu* and *Ammi* got married and *Amma Nani* too passed away, *Nanphu* moved to Aligarh, to Mishkat, the home of *Ammi's* youth, so we could go there and relive *Ammi's* life to understand why she is different. When *Babajaan* went on a year's assignment to Libya, *Mammijan* moved in with *Nanphu*.

"That was 35 years ago, Azad," said *Nanphu,* after a very long pause, visibly debilitated by her emotional discourse. "You have heard much about Sara's illness and you will continue to learn about it in years to come; much more than I can ever tell. But there are some things you will not learn from outside and these I must tell you, so you know what makes her so strong, how she manages to stay well for such long periods of time, and why many of us derive our strength from her."

That was to be a story for another day, which was never told. When I returned, *Ammi* met me at the airport in Bangalore. *Nanphu* had passed away a few hours after I left Aligarh. As I sat in the car beside *Ammi*, she held my hand. I could feel the strength coursing through her veins, but do not know where this strength came from.

Sara thereafter —

Catharsis of grief

Once amid the soft silver sadness in the sky
There came a man of fortune, a drifter passing by
He moved with some uncertainty, as if he didn't know
Just what he was there for, or where he ought to go
Once he reached for something golden hanging from a tree
And his hand came down empty

Carole King

Abba was a brilliant man, a mental giant. He had shifting moods and a fantastic sense of humour, and he was generous to a fault. I have heard him roar like a lion when some poor sod in the accounts department of the university attempted to make him compromise his principles. I have also heard him whinge and cry like a child. There was an endearing smile tucked in at one corner of his mouth, which could turn sarcastic in just a moment. He listened to Beethoven and Mozart and Tchaikovsky and Bach on his Grundig spool player and tunelessly sang at the top of his voice. He was not an engineer, not a designer, not an architect, but he was a visionary who created Mishkat. Mishkat was not just our home, it was a phenomenon in our lives, in the lives of many.

Abba woke up at four in the morning and took a cold shower, summer or winter, and then sat at his typewriter, whose loud clickety-clicks shattered the dawn. Of course everyone woke up then, and he made tea for the adults and *joshanda,* a bitter sweet, slightly soapy, medicinal brew made from some intriguing ingredients, to clear sinuses, for those of us he deemed not yet adults. All his life he gave me a cup of *joshanda.* Now you can buy *Hamdard ka Joshina* in a bottle, but in no way does it pack the same punch. While *Amma* had a leisurely morning,

Abba cooked a hot breakfast for the large family; quite odd in an Indian household; and then he was ready to go. He was always dressed in dapper fashion, whether in *khadi,* handspun and handwoven, or serge, a type of twill fabric; whether in a *sherwani,* a long, collarless coat, or a three-piece suit, complete with a dashing tie. Every night he used to polish every one of his several shoes and there was a spring in his step reflected in the shining polish of his shoes.

But I never really knew him very well, never knew what was in his heart and mind, never knew what made him tick or what would snuff him out. He communicated with us through our mother, *Amma*, who was the steady influence in our lives during our growing years and for me, even later. She was very strict with us, in how we talked or dressed or sat or thought, and it was very much later that I realised that some of it came from *Abba*, through her. *Abba* never had the time to interact with us much. He was forever on the run, living by the railway timetable, travelling on university work, his mind racing all the while on larger problems of the world; until one day he just ran out of life itself. Which is why, finding him looking so remote and still, swathed in the pure white *kafan,* shroud, unhinged my mind. That night, they carried him in a procession to the burial ground past the Medical College Hospital that had not been able to save him, the people in the *janaza,* the funeral procession, carrying flashlights against the thick, impenetrable darkness of that terrible night and the poor lighting. I watched from our terrace and am now aware of feelings and emotions I did not experience as I smoked my one last cigarette of the day; up on the second terrace, hidden by the large overhead water tank, I watched the flashlights converge at a point in the too near burial ground.

I must have cried, as I do cry when moved by pain and sadness. Trying to accept that he was no more was very painful, but I don't remember any of that. There was no overwhelming sadness, no urge to cry, no compulsion to be brave. I completely skipped Kübler-Ross's stages of grief. There was no denial, only very slight anger at unrelated events;

I did not bargain with the almighty that *Abba* be somehow returned to us; I was not depressed, in that I did not stay in bed or mope around. I bathed, dressed, talked, read, almost from the next day onwards, as I saw *Amma* go through these motions too. She was a strong person and so did not need to go through these stages to arrive at an acceptance of what had happened and of its consequences; she instantly accepted with grit and grace. I suppose I did not accept, did not take ownership of this indelible reality, although I did not deny it either. What I do remember is a strange quiet descended upon me. I have always thought that was my way of grieving, or coping without grief, and I know it was not depression in the way I have experienced it later. My soul was not depleted, my spirit not shattered. It seemed an unconscious resolve to step off the bandwagon of accepted, normal sequences of emotion and climb onto a manic, hurtling conveyor belt of totally different realities; as what was to follow from here on was my reality; however unreal it may have seemed to others.

It was some weeks after *Abba* died; somewhere deep inside my being I began to fantasise, to build a world and a life that was less painful than the one I was living in, that would make me feel something other than the dull, lifeless ache. Every thought is etched deeply in my mind and even in retrospect it does not seem all that strange. I left behind my family's minimal values, the fairly spartan living, and dreamt of luxuries that were grand. I went and deposited our family belongings with *Nanphu, Abba's* sister, in Lucknow. They say I started to fall apart there; but I know I had started to fall apart much earlier, even as I showed a brave and sane front. I took a jeep ride to and from Delhi. On the way to Delhi I hung out of the jeep with the wind in my face and hair, but that was the only movement. The still, grey asphalt of the road just flashed by in dull strips. In Delhi I walked around CP and visited many handloom, handicraft and jewellery shops, looking for things to make myself and my surroundings more beautiful, luxurious things which I could not afford; but that did not seem to matter. On the way back to Aligarh this same asphalt came alive with deep, vibrant colours and resonating sounds, sucking me in to become the central character in what seemed like reality for the moment, and for a long while after. When I reached Aligarh I came out of my silence and gave expression to these hallucinations and delusions of grandeur as I have learnt to call them since.

I can quite imagine how much getting used to it must have taken the rest of the family, who were only just learning to cope without *Abba's* decisive guidance. At that time, however, I was completely unaware of any dilemma except those centred around me and my perception of what was important. For some reason, looks were of paramount importance.

My older sister, *Apia,* found me sitting on the floor of my room, dressed in her magenta *gharara,* a dress described by Azad, part of her wedding trousseau; with my face, neck and hands softened with one of her lotions. Was I under the illusion that I was getting married? Or was it someone else who was getting married? Or was it some other celebration? There were hollowed out sounds of merriment in the sultry air, the pattering of feet running up and down the stairs and the light in my room was too bright. When she came in, I asked her, "Have you ever lived in a commune, *Apia*?" and this quite bewildered her. I do not quite recall why I asked her this question; I do recall however that this question was inextricably linked to the muffled sounds of celebration in the stairwell.

Very quietly *Apia* packed the bottle of lotion with my belongings to take to hospital. For a family that argued a lot, I am amazed at the unquestioning consensus to seek immediate medical intervention, and deeply grateful for it.

The next day there was again a jeep ride back to Delhi. I don't remember very much at all, not even whom I was with; my brother Kamran tells me it was he, *Apia* and *Amma* who took me to Delhi. All I can remember is that the alive asphalt was still there. I, however, remained in a catatonic state throughout the ride, through the wait in some lobby, recognising and ignoring the hushed conversations, being heralded into a bare room with two beds and a small table, where finally, *Amma* and I were left alone for several hours. My bed sheet had MIH printed on it. This was spread the wrong side up, so it read HIM. I refused to even sit on my bed, saying it was a male bed and they had put us in the wrong room. The entire night I spent curled up at the foot of the other bed that was meant for *Amma* to sleep on.

I woke up in the night to go to the bathroom and discovered that my underwear was stained red. I had started my period, but I did not know what it was. When I did not come back into the room for a long while, *Amma* came to look for me. She helped me wear a pad as she had done ten years ago, back in 7 Shibli Road when I was eleven. Tintin *Apa*, my youngest aunt, took away my soiled clothes to wash.

Later I was told that I was at a big government hospital in Delhi and the people around me were psychiatrists and psychiatric students; it was their resting room that we were to live in, as *Amma* did not want to subject me to the real psychiatric ward. This was a whole other time when you could make such a request and have it granted. I look back on *Amma* in amazement and awe. In her I discovered a solid, diminutive giant, a stalwart, one who was so much more than a mild university professor and a strict parent, recently widowed. When my friend Adil and I came back together in our mid-20s, she became his steadfast friend, a friendship that changed some over the years, as he and I changed our relationship, but which both he and she cherished throughout her life. I know they have talked much about me and that helped her pass away peacefully in '99 and has helped Adil hold on to his sanity over all these troubled years.

The doctors diagnosed me as an Affective Schizoid, but I did not know that until almost a year later, when I found the discharge slip in *Amma's* bag and then did not really know what it meant until I could read up on it. Now when I search the internet for this term I cannot find it. The closest I have come to it is Schizoaffective disorder.

I was in the hospital for five or six weeks, maybe more, the turbulence of my mind projected as hallucinatory images in all sorts of settings, superimposed on the dull, coloured walls of the hospital corridors. I would run up and down stairs, in the corridors and grounds of the hospital, just run till I could run no more and start again the following day. I have tried to pin down my thoughts as I ran; these thoughts were racing too, keeping pace with me. The thoughts were not connected or rational and I recall making quantum leaps from one thought to another; though I cannot tell now what each parcel of thoughts was made up of. Kamran stayed with me during the day while *Amma* rested in JNU, and I was free to roam anywhere in the hospital as long as he was with me. He just remembers being completely exhausted by the explosion of my physical and mental energy. The way Mariam must have been exhausted when I spun her around when we were little girls.

Some of Adil and my schoolmates were interns at that hospital. Their *neem hakeem khatre jaan,* partial medical knowledge – a threat to life, led them to conjecture and draw their own half-baked conclusions from what they saw, which angered *Amma* very much. Specially when she found out that one of the psychiatrists played tennis with one of my schoolmates and actually discussed me with him as they volleyed. Confidentiality is a very loose principle for most. Many years later when *Amma* expressed concern about this I realised, with surprise, that I couldn't care less who knew. Much larger and more fundamental issues were at stake.

Down several flights of stairs from my room, we came to the ground floor. Stepping out into a bright pool of sunshine brought us to a small stall that sold magazines and newspapers, beside which a chilli pepper red car was parked. A young man attended at the counter, but I could clearly see another man under the counter, crouched on his haunches, wearing a dirty white cambric *kurta,* a long collarless shirt, and wide *Lucknavi* pyjamas. I could see the top of his head with thick, black hair, and arms that were wrapped around his drawn up knees, into which he buried his face. Every day I went to the stall with Kamran, who watched me sit down and talk to this person for hours. Kamran told me several times that there was no one under the counter, but I disregarded him and thought him blind. One day the counter got dislodged and fell to the ground. There was no one there. It did not bother me that he was gone, raised no questions in my mind. The drugs were working and I had begun learning the art of practised indifference to relatedness; relatedness to people, events and pain. From that day on, the red hot chilli pepper Honda Civic was no longer parked by the stall, and I had *Amma* buy me a knitting magazine I have never opened, only because there was a pattern in it of a sweater that I thought would look good on me.

The doctors were very disturbing to my already disturbed mind. I was a psychologist's daughter and had also studied an introductory course in psychology during my undergraduate years; I was, therefore, familiar with all the terminology. The head psychiatrist was a lady known to Tintin *Apa*. She would come to the door of my room and her brood of psychiatry students would crowd around the door. They would ask me questions, which most often, *Amma* answered. Then they would start a discussion and I could hear, "The patient this... and the patient that..." By now they had started me on some medication and this was beginning to have its initial effect. My mind was still running away, but on leaden feet. I tolerated this babble for a while; then one day I lost it. Once again they had all taken up position at the door, but before they could hurl their first question at me, I began to shout in a low, menacing voice, "Hey you, get the hell out of here! Shit! Don't take another step into my room. I am not 'the patient.' I am Sara. If you don't have the decency to call me by my name when you talk to me, if you don't know that it is impolite to talk about a person in her presence, if you want to talk at me instead of to me – then I want to have nothing to do with you. Just get out, go, go!" I had not discovered 'fuck' until then. I looked the head psychiatrist squarely in the eyes and said, "You brutes! Teach them to be human beings first, or maybe you should teach yourself that." I was just short of 21 years old, five feet, two inches tall and weighed 38 kilograms, but there must have been some weight in what I said, because the whole lot hastily retreated, never to return. It is said that I was normally not angry, especially not with people whom I trusted; except once, when I refused to take my medicines and Kamran had to pin me down by my wrist and the attendant had to force feed me the pills. A wonderful young doctor was assigned to me, instead of the gaggling bunch. I was very ill, with not a rational thought in my mind, so it would not have mattered which doctor saw me on standard hospital rounds. However, much remained of what this reserved and polite young man said to me, especially when I went back as an outpatient; and this I listened to and carried back to Aligarh. I count him as my first psychiatrist. He was Dr SS.

In this time they tried all kinds of drugs on me, but nothing worked and my hallucinations continued unabated. The two drugs I remember being given, at different times, were Largactil and Haldol or Haloperidol, both from the dopamine antagonist class of medicines (I don't really know what that means. I got it from the internet some years back when they wanted to prescribe Haldol again in Sweden.), that act as antipsychotics and are used in the treatment of schizophrenia and other acute psychotic states. These were aided by sedatives and tranquilisers whose names I have since forgotten.

When nothing worked and my state seemed to be getting more and more acute and pronounced, the doctors took *Amma* aside and had a long conference with her in hushed tones. My exhausted mind did not even want to know what they were talking about. Then they sent me into a brightly lit, very stark and clinical room, and gave me an intravenous injection in the back of my hand; I blacked out. I had walked to this room with Kamran, but was brought out on a stretcher. (When I was eight years old I had an eye operation for squint. Then too, I walked to and into the operation theatre independently and scolded an assistant doctor for trying to have me taken from the ward on a stretcher. "Why? When I am awake and my legs work just fine?") They repeated this on three consecutive days I think; or maybe four. I don't know for how long I passed out each time. The treatment was followed by intense headaches and nausea. *Amma* massaged my temples and the back of my head with coconut oil, as I retched into a pail. On the last day, when the headache subsided, I realised I had snapped out of it and my mind could no longer camouflage the dingy passageway of the government hospital and transform it into an art gallery. The *ghubaar,* the dust, had lifted off my mind. I turned twenty one.

What they did in the room was Electroconvulsive Therapy (ECT), or shock treatment, in layman's terms. Thankfully it was under general anaesthesia, not so thankfully I too imagine it only from the movies I have seen, with bodies convulsing wildly. I would not want to actually experience and remember what it feels like to have an electric current course through me, as my body convulses. For many years I did not know what it was that they did to me in that room. I did not ask and just assumed it was the injection in the back of my hand that was the whole treatment. I only came to know five years later, during the next attack of this illness, that I had been treated with ECT.

The prior discussion with *Amma* was to explain the procedure to her and also to apprise her of possible memory loss. I forget if it was loss of long term or short term memory, and whether the loss was supposed to be short-lived or long term/permanent. I do know that the possibility of memory loss so terrified *Amma* that she even contemplated not giving her permission. I used to wonder why she was always testing what I could remember. I thought perhaps it was because she did not want me to remember my psychotic state; it was my turn to be perplexed when it pleased her that I had forgotten nothing.

The episode was of schizophrenic proportions, especially with the intense visual, aural and sensory hallucinations, which I can perceive even now in my mind and memory, and it was treated as such. There was no discussion of a mood disorder or manic depression. It is possible that the doctors were only looking at the extreme, acute symptoms presented upon my arrival at the hospital, and treated these mainly with antipsychotics, because that was the urgency. No one was really listening to accounts of perfect normalcy before this episode. This was not slight or even severe depression; it was not merely hypomanic or manic energy that made me run around doing things; it was not an extreme state of happiness. I was in the grip of extreme psychosis that had completely deranged my thought. This they had perhaps seen only in someone with some sort of schizophrenia of the affect. Once I regained consciousness and came out of the following depression, I never went back to the doctors in Delhi. Perhaps I should have, to show them my nonpsychotic side. Euthymic is the word. I would have liked my young doctor in Delhi to see my euthymic state.

I forgot nothing, not my hallucinations nor what the doctors said in my hearing, not the expressions of hope and despondency that crossed *Amma's* face dozens of times a day, the feeling of timelessness, the fear of abnormality, the hatred for the psychiatrists – there are so many things I did not forget, but there are at least two that I did. One was the feeling of normalcy where emotions and feelings were concerned, any feelings; and the other was, not the fact that *Abba* had died but that his death had caused me pain. I could finally recall normalcy of emotions in some measure and simulate it, but I could never recall the pain that was associated with *Abba's* passing away; perhaps for fear that I may relive it. This fear stands today. I think *Amma* sensed that I did not really want to talk about *Abba* as I came to terms with what had happened to me.

I insist that the period before my first mental breakdown is one of grieving and cannot be termed depression. However, I had a very dark period of depression immediately following this episode, for over a year afterwards. No one has been able to explain to me if these intense bouts of depression are a natural follow on from the psychotic highs or if they are drug induced, where the drug does not know when to stop acting and keeps plunging me down. One doctor I discussed this with suggested it may be a bit of both.

One disturbing memory I have is of a period of time during this year of dark despair when Hindu Muslim riots broke out in Aligarh and the rioting was too close for comfort. The market next door was burnt and Muslims were on the rampage against Hindu shop owners in retaliation for what Hindus had done to them in the city area, across the railway lines. There were stories of mutilated bodies being found in nearby gutters. As revenge, the Hindus were planning to attack from behind the Medical College Colony, from a place called *Dhoharra*. People were collecting stones and bricks on their terraces against the contingency of this attack.

A young friend came via the back lanes to sit by *Amma.* In low tones he would describe preparing bodies for burial or cremation. Sometimes the bodies were so mutilated they could barely tell if it was a man or a woman, but they could always tell when it was a child and many children were massacred. Randomly they prepared the bodies for burial or cremation; as apart from circumcision in males they had no way of telling whether the person was a Muslim or a Hindu. He would then invariably go out into the courtyard and retch for a long time, on a stomach empty of food, before *Amma* could get some tea and toast into him. The mental image of en masse death was so dehumanising and frightening. I know my mind created some of these images for me, but they were born of a terrible reality. Those were intense times and the intensity permeated the thick darkness of the abyss I was in. There was round-the-clock curfew for as long as 72 hours sometimes, so there was no physical escape either, and darkness brought with it not the solace of sleep but sounds that conjured up images in the mind. Were these hallucinations then? I used to stay close to *Amma*, drawing comfort and courage from her calm sanity.

After the rioting had peaked and gone down a little, *Amma* asked me if she could go to Chandigarh for a few days, to be part of the selection committee for someone's appointment in the university there. I said she could, but started to worry even before she left. My brother and sister and the two cousins who lived with us at the time, endlessly played cards. For that one time in my life I joined them and incessantly played court piece while listening to music on a small, blue cassette player. The concentration needed for a game I did not know how to play and the loud music helped to drown out the sounds in my head, so my mind did not have much to base its images on. What were these sounds and images? When my mind is all wired up I still listen to music continuously to drown out sounds that have become loud and taken on new forms. But then I hear new sounds in the music as well, that were not there before. Auditory hallucinations have many possible sources, but to see and touch a person or a thing, where none is, is something I am still unable to fathom. It is these images that I see, like on a cinema screen or in a play, but ones in which I step outside of myself and participate in, while standing by and watching them too. It is as though my self splits into two, especially when I am in the noisy, superfast zone of my affect, but sometimes in the stillness and silence of extreme depression too. The part of me that enters the unreal world is able to step back into reality when I am well again. However, there is that part of me that stands in the no man's land in between reality and unreality and watches. That part stays with me, with crystal clear memories and images of what is not real, and this part never reenters reality again. In any case, for this part of my psyche there is no distinction between the real and the unreal as others perceive it.

Everything from then on became dull and lifeless. I could not string together letters of the alphabet to make words and forgot how to read completely. *Mamoon Saheb, Amma's* brother, took leave to spend time with me and teach me how to read, a task that was nearly impossible. I bloated up so, my head and neck were like a cylinder; I sat folded over my stomach and there was a big bump on a hunched back. I was in deep, suicidal depression. Trying to speak was a nightmare and I used to agonise if I had to say a few words. I was in this state when Adil's older brother asked him to come and see me, and he did, bringing another friend, my distant cousin. I spent two days rehearsing what I would say to them, but to no avail. *Amma* put a *charpai,* a woven bed, out for us in the winter sun, and a couple of chairs. I sat in one of those chairs without talking, without blinking, without any expression or feeling, even without thinking. Adil and my cousin talked non-stop, with an awkwardness that lent an urgency to everything they said, and when they ran out of things to say, they left, rather abruptly. I was acutely and unemotionally aware that something was not right, but did not have even an iota of feeling in me to bring the dull ache out to the fore to make me miserable. These were all emotions I had forgotten, including anger and happiness.

It was later that year when I discovered the hospital discharge slip where the diagnosis in the discharge summary read Affective Schizoid. None of us ever gave a name to what had happened to me, almost as though not giving it a name would perhaps make the illness cease to exist; such is the power of nomenclature. I quickly jammed the discharge slip back into *Amma's* bag where I had found it and no one but *Amma* and I knew that my illness had a name. We never spoke about it to each other.

Amma and I spent a lot of time together after *Abba* died, during and after my first episode. We travelled too, to London, to Calpe in Spain and to New York and Oklahoma in the US. We learnt a lot about each other, from each other and learnt to talk once again about *Abba*, tentatively at first, but then with growing confidence. It is then that *Amma* started describing to me how *Abba* was, aboard an ocean liner bringing us home from Canada. He started believing that there were men on the ship who were after him, who were spying on him. In random conversations on the ship he could hear his name mentioned. They were following him to his cabin down below. It was because he had leftist leanings and it was part of some big plot to destroy him. Earlier he had been granted a visa to travel to the US, but before he could walk out, his passport was snatched back and the visa cancelled by multiple stamps. They gave no reason, but it was quite evident that *Abba's* progressive outlook was working against him. Perhaps this was the trigger for his breakdown; *Amma* thought it might be so. We were all very young at that time except *Apia,* and when I spoke to her about this many years after my own breakdowns, she said she too could remember some of this episode when he took her to Paris.

According to *Amma*, *Abba* never saw a doctor. By sheer dint of will power and a strong belief in himself, he brought his thoughts under control. It took time but he was well again. With just books on psychology to help him, he diagnosed himself as a paranoid schizophrenic and set about profiling himself for the future. That was the second time I heard a term from the fat Abnormal Psychology textbook applied to a real person, and it frightened me. Abnormal Psychology had suddenly become more real than what I had bargained for.

I knew what *Amma* was trying to tell me, but I did not want to hear it, did not want it to become my reality. As first year BSc students, Kamran and I had picked up this very book any number of times to stealthily enter the dark world of mental aberrations and felt a vicarious thrill when some small part applied to us. Very soon I would study Abnormal Psychology in graduate school. I wanted to maintain an objective stance and be a bystander, but a connection had been made and I was inexorably bound to my father by genetics. Over the years I have realised what a powerful factor genetics is; but I have also come to believe that the hereditary stronghold, that cannot perhaps be broken, can possibly be loosened enough by the environment you create around you to allow you a chance at healthy normalcy. I do believe this normalcy has to be redefined and will always sit at the edge of fire. Also it is something that has to be allowed by significant others in your life. When I went to Mishkat in 1999, I found, amongst *Abba's* books, the Layman's Guide to Psychiatry by James A Brussel, and brought it back with me. Kamran commented that psychiatry must have come a long way since James Brussel MD, and I may want to pick up a more modern book of the same type if I wanted to get more information. But I did not want up-to-date information on psychiatry, I just wanted to know what guidelines *Abba* had used to heal himself.

That despondent year passed slowly, painfully, and I could not attend university to complete my MSc in Chemistry. I could not read despite *Mamoon Saheb's* continued efforts to help me grapple with the semantics and syntax of words and sentences. The time was not right and my mind was still in the throes of psychoses and antipsychotics. Much of the year I spent huddled on the terrace, whether cold, hot, or rainy, smoking *beedis,* rolled up tobacco leaf, or cigarette stubs when I could not lay hands on a whole cigarette. There was nowhere to go and nothing to do. When the blankness and emptiness became all-encompassing, the only thought that would enter my mind is that of suicide. It was a faraway thought, a comforting thought that told me there was a way out when things became unbearable. Strangely enough this was just a thought and not a perceived reality, fortunately not even a remotely possible reality. Yet, I had looked for ways to end my life. Those were not the days of the internet so I must have found a book on poisonous chemicals in the department library. I homed in on mercury, as the book had a whole chapter devoted to mercury poisoning and the terrible ways in which you would die if you ingested more than a certain amount. In *Amma's* dressing room stood a chest of drawers, our old chest of drawers where we kept our clothes as children, and where Mariam's cat gave birth to kittens long ago. In the top, right drawer *Amma* kept passports and other important papers, plus her few pieces of jewellery and the piece of gold she had once brought from Kuwait. In the back, right corner of this drawer stood a large test tube of mercury with a black rubber bung. I can swear I have picked it up in my hands and noted how heavy it was, I have noticed its inverted convex meniscus, and then I have kept it back. I never pulled out the stopper, touched the mercury or spoke about it to anyone. It never struck me as odd that *Amma* should have a test tube of mercury in her drawer. Some time later it was not there. Today I know it was never there. My mind had conjured up the perfect illusion of a terrible reality, an eventuality that it never wanted me to face. It is after many years and many mental breakdown cycles that I begin to recognise how powerful the mind is.

This whole year is coloured grey in my memory, with little variation of shade. Adil met me only once during this time and he remembers doing so too. I have no idea how he felt, as we have never really spoken about it; perhaps pity, maybe even sympathy, but he could not have felt empathy; he had no cognitive schema, no close call with such a state in another human being, nor in himself, and it would have been difficult for him to place himself in my shoes. He waited until we could communicate about books and music to come near me again, but I have always marvelled that he did at all and often sought me out even though I was not really ready for any kind of relationship. The fact that he saw me in this horrific mental and emotional state, physical too as I was just a plasmic mass, and still wanted to come close to me is the one thing I hold in deep gratitude and it has kept us together. Because, I would have you believe me, there is nothing commonplace or everyday about this illness, and its ugliness is repulsive and hard to ignore. Still, at this point Adil had not seen this horror in its entirety, and there were times in later years when he would cringe at every onslaught. But that was much, much later. Even as I was getting to know him afresh, to find out that he listened to Bob Dylan and not Abba, as he was sharing the books he read with my *Amma, Mamoon Saheb* and me, I decided to leave everything and go to the US to study several aspects of Psychology. Adil was in the US too, but we never met.

For the five years following my first episode I only thought of schizophrenia and studied all its ramifications. I tried to relate to my sketchy understanding of it. I did not think of *Abba* much or the fact that I may have inherited an illness from him. Slowly I started thinking of this illness as something triggered by the shock of his death, and now that the shock had receded, so had the illness. Thus, none of us were prepared for the second episode that came in the US. The American doctors completely changed the diagnosis and my life from then on was set on a path of understanding and acceptance, of a different self and a different reality.

Hurtling forward

Slow down, you move too fast
You got to make the morning last

Simon and Garfunkel

The first episode was followed by terribly deep depression, but even then I did not descend to the pits. I did not harm myself or take my life. Despite the depth of despair, despite not having a concept of the next moment, leave alone a tomorrow, in spite of failed coordination so that food in the hand sometimes did not reach the mouth, despite not being able to read or talk, despite not being able to relate to even a single individual, despite the hopelessness that comes when no emotion can be expressed or even felt, despite so many negative factors too numerous to recall and mention, there was a tiny seed of positive energy inside that even I did not know existed. That strain of positive energy I recognise only in retrospect, and it has pulled me out then and in every subsequent episode. Some of the episodes have been followed by depression of severe intensity, when any physical or mental movement was well-nigh impossible and I would cower from any human contact. Now I know that eventually I come out of it.

Once the drugs were withdrawn and their effect began to wear off, some of my shaken, crumbling or lost confidence started to return and I wanted to live again. I completed my MSc in Chemistry, but that was only to prove a point; I was very sure I did not want to study Chemistry any further.

I went to the Chemistry department every day. On my cycle, I came out of the gate of Mishkat, crossed the Medical College Road and cut across a large, bare field. At the other end of the field was a small gate into Minto E, the university graveyard. I would dismount from the cycle and wheel it through the graveyard, then mount it at the gate at the other end, and go on my way. I never went near *Abba's* grave. A bent old man used to watch me.

One day he stopped me, *"Yahaan kyun aati ho, bitiya,"* why do you come here, child? I told him my father lay buried here and he said, *"Beti, apne waalid ki yaadein apne dil mein saja ke rakho, yahan mat aaya karo,"* my daughter, decorate the memories of your father in your heart, don't come here. *Amma* never visited Minto E, although in addition to *Abba,* two of her brothers were laid to rest there. Her *rickshaw* took the long way round to the Education department. Mariam chose *Abba's* epitaph, a Mirza Ghalib *sher:*

Sab kahaan kuch lala-o-gul mein numaayan ho gaeen
Khak mein kya suratein hongi ke pinhan ho gaeen

Not all, only a few appear in roses and tulips,
What faces there must be that were buried in the ashes.

But I am not sure if she saw it writ on *Abba's* tombstone. We were mourning a loss that we had not yet fully accepted and so we were shy of *qabr parasti* or worship at the grave and not yet ready to celebrate a life in the *Sufi* tradition.

A schoolmate, a year senior, came to be in my final year Physical Chemistry class, to complete his MSc. If I had lost a year, he had lost two. During the course of the year he disappeared from class several times and I heard that he had some mental illness for which he was being treated. His father came home once and had a long discussion with *Amma* behind closed doors. I passed my exams but don't know if he did. Some time later I found out that he was no more. I don't know the circumstances of his death and have never asked anyone. As I sat in our class of four students, I had wondered though what was troubling him and what medical treatment he was getting for it. For me he remains an unassuming, gentle person, but one whose mind and body were in the throes of some terrible illness and the drugs to treat it.

My newfound awareness of the mind raised many questions that I wanted to make the subject of study. Still, I was afraid of plunging straight into Abnormal Psychology. Some part of me had decided that there was nothing abnormal about me. What had happened to me was because of the grave shock of *Abba's* untimely death. The severity of what happened to me was not of the norm, but not abnormal either. And this will not happen again. *Amma* encouraged this belief, though not explicitly. As a safe medium, I decided to bring my *Abba* and *Amma's* disciplines together and study the psychology of learning. Aligarh began to stifle me and, as a well-meaning professor began to pull me towards doctoral work in Biochemistry, I suddenly had visions of never being able to get away; so I decided to cut and run. A handloom and handicraft store in the Connaught Place area of the Delhi of my youthful dreams, seemed a safe distance away, both physically and emotionally. It was a most arduous six months working as a salesperson at this shop and staying at a working women's hostel nearby. Adil lost his elder brother during this time and I had to take a hold of my sanity even as I grieved with him, but could not shed tears.

It was an unreal life, far removed from anything I had known, folding bed covers, hanging clothes, dusting the shelves, keeping accounts, battling the *hijras,* eunuchs, at closing time; but it saved me from a PhD in Biochemistry. I started seriously thinking about further studies and began writing a statement of purpose that would get me into graduate school in the fields of Education and Psychology. Whatever minimal understanding I had of my mental illness, relearning how to read, dining table discussions of Education and Psychology with my parents, reading books from their bookshelf, the undergraduate course in beginning Psychology; all found their way into my statement and lent substance to my purpose.

In the autumn of 1982 I went to the US for graduate studies in Education and Psychology, but coming from a background in Chemistry, it was quite a lateral shift and a challenge. I do not have a copy of my statement of purpose any more, but I remember it being very precise in intent and quite convincing in its arguments that I be allowed to study Education and Psychology, although I had only studied pure sciences until then. A university in the US gave me admission in their Master of Education programme in Elementary and Early Childhood Education, and there began a wonderful year, studying invigorating courses that I had only imagined and that had nothing to do with Chemistry! It is there that the possibility of facilitating the learning of children took root. My passion for this new learning was all-consuming; every assignment became a research paper, every discussion a discourse and I became a sponge for knowledge and understanding.

Initially it was quite unsettling finding suitable housing and I got into some fairly undesirable situations with people, mainly American boys of varying backgrounds, whom I shared housing with. I was also stranded without transport several times in fairly shady parts of town. Finally, a lovely couple from Rajasthan sublet me a room of their married student housing on campus, and right from the start I knew all would be well. I became part of the quiet rhythm of a domestic life without any pretensions or stress. The wife, Neelu, taught me how to make *daal bati* and *rotis*; the first *roti* was always for the gods, she said, and it went straight from the fire to the garbage bin. In exchange I taught her how to speak English. This simple woman from my country made all the difference and I felt I belonged in this strange, new place.

Looking back I can see that as winter closed in, the street lights had an unusual brightness and a mesmerising effect, and I roamed the campus on winged feet, or went round and round on the three campus bus, in which the sudden silence would tell me I was again talking loudly to myself and gesticulating expansively. Were these indicators of what would come? Losing my way in town or being bullied by a male housemate, who shoved his knife scar in my face, were really nothing compared to losing *Abba* and being mentally stranded in a no man's land of illusions, delusions and hallucinations. I, therefore, never made a connection. Winter passed in this slightly elevated state and I soon became restless. One day I suddenly left this university before the academic year was out, leaving my Master's incomplete. I moved to another university, in Illinois, where my sister Mariam and her husband Roby were. When the second incident of whatever mental illness I was supposed to have occurred, I was in this Illinois university, living with Mariam and Roby and working towards a PhD in Educational Psychology. The recognition of my own potential in, as yet uncharted waters, the year before was a very heady experience and I had already begun to enter an unreal world by the time I arrived here in the summer of 1983. The early part of that summer was spent in convincing the Chemistry department to give me a teaching assistantship in Chemistry, so I could pursue graduate studies in Educational Psychology. Everyone told me I was a fool to believe that would happen, but I was sure it would, and it did! The Head of Chemistry must have seen beyond my reckless bravado, to the single minded purpose, and she called the professor of Educational Psychology working in the area of Motivation and Achievement. They were concerned about setting a precedence, but something must have told them it may not be a worthless endeavour. And so I started with a quarter-time teaching assistantship, teaching Chem 100 to a bunch of totally uninterested kids, studying all sorts of unrelated subjects. Did the professors really see something special in me to make this exception, or were these early signs of some sort of delusion that I was able to so convincingly transfer to the decision makers? I have many examples of this, where thoughts and actions that are labelled delusions of grandeur are also recognised and accepted by others. Why would they do that if I am only deluding myself and there is no fraction of truth in this delusion?

Anyway, for the rest of the summer Mariam and I went to *Apia's,* and our time was spent converting junk into artefacts and pieces of art. *Amma* came to spend time with us. These were calm weeks, but now I see that the calmness was an illusion and I was already getting detached from reality, in a creatively channelled, hyperactive way. The preceding year in the US had shown me clearly what was possible and what was not, in my educational pursuits and my personal life respectively, and this knowledge had come at a heavy price, which had begun to churn my mind even before I left the earlier university.

As I have often explained to my youngest, Rumi, when he says he is only feeling good and what could be so bad about this, is that for people in our situation, feeling good may just be an emotional storm brewing, as our mental makeup does not know just how much good to feel and when to stop. As a recent doctor explained to him and me, for baseline normalcy or euthymia to be maintained, we can be mildly glad for extended periods of time or even explicitly happy for some time, given that there is known reason for this happiness and we take breaks from it. Beyond this, given strong reason, we can experience elation for a few hours or be momentarily euphoric. The state of ecstasy is only allowed in the instance of a deep spiritual or religious experience. I have experienced all in the span of a single episode and even outside an episode. So the question is whether an episode is some sort of a spiritual experience, albeit one that comes from deep within and we don't know it to be that. No, that does not sound right, but for a moment I wanted to believe it.

Things came to a head during the winter of 1983–1984 and I started to feel irrationally marginalised by Mariam and Roby's friends, which engendered sentiments of anger and resentment. I was also paranoid about our combined financial situation and not confident of Mariam and Roby's capability to manage our finances without bankrupting us. I remember being on the phone a lot, mainly to cousins, talking about my situation. My classes, both the ones I attended in Educational Psychology and the ones I taught in beginning Chemistry, took on a strange surreal quality. I was glib in talk, whether explaining Chemistry or delivering a discourse on some aspect of the psychology of learning. Getting good grades was effortless and my students adored me. My Chemistry professor wrote that I was impressively Socratic in my teaching methodology. At home, I could churn out 50 *aloo parathas* or flatbread made with a potato stuffing, single-handedly, downing several potent drinks at the same time. I was also introduced to the 'bong,' a neat little *huqqah* or water pipe for smoking large amounts of weed. I lived as though there was no tomorrow, and suddenly there really was no tomorrow, not even a today.

Only now, after many, many years of living with this illness, I know something is wrong when I feel this way. But at that time I didn't. My first episode had no preceding intensification of negative emotions of this kind or a simple gladness fast taking on ecstatic proportions. Actually, there was a depth to my grieving then, that made me tuned to emotions in a different way and was its own kind of a high, born of extreme sadness. This was different, it was sustained elation bordering on euphoria, and I had no way of knowing that I was making a quantum leap into a mental and emotional state of a whole other dimension. Whatever information I had, pointed to schizophrenia, and my understanding of it was that it is a continuously disturbed state, not with such highs and lows. As I was not continuously disturbed and many features of schizophrenia were missing from my symptoms altogether, outside the earlier hospitalised phase, I discounted it as a possible diagnosis. No one had, until then, spoken of manic depression.

Snow had begun to fall by the time my mental state started to affect my life and became apparent to others. I became increasingly intense about things, but also abandoned. We went up north to listen to a concert and I sang L-O-L-A Lola all the way back, slip sliding away in the snow to the tune of the song, when walking home from the parking lot. I had much to say and was not shy of saying it. Later people told me how they tried to avoid me, but I would not let them go away. Sometimes I was quiet, but that was because words would not precipitate. The words were all there, bottled up inside. One evening I was closest to being depressed. There was no one at home and I was wandering about, when I walked to the kitchen window and looked out. Someone had carved out FUCK YOU in the snow on the bonnet of a car and it felt as though someone had shouted out the two words at me. It kept ringing in my ears and the letters would not leave my sight as I stumbled back into the living room and crouched on the green sofa. Several hours had passed when I got up and called our friend Nick to say I wanted to write; he immediately ran in with his typewriter. He pulled up his knees and sat on the ground in the corner of our living room, and watched me for hours and hours as I poured out my soul into his little electric typewriter. It came out as an extremely long scroll of paper. I have no idea today what I wrote, but at that time it was my PhD thesis. Someone safely put away this long scroll of paper that had expressions of my reformatted thoughts, deformed beyond recognition.

Days rolled seamlessly into nights, and nights were thrown back into days, without the relief of sleep. I was all wired and shaking, but unable even to see the need of correcting this state of affairs. When five or six days had passed like this, Mariam and Roby felt that something was definitely wrong; they were, however, totally out of their depth and called *Apia*. *Apia* arrived on that cold Illinois winter day in January 1984. She brought with her Haldol, so my mind and body could have some rest and she tells me I slept a little. I had already been awake round-the-clock for almost a week straight. We had tried to get some sleeping aid from the university clinic, but they refused, despite being told that I had psychiatric problems. They, in turn, offered me Benadryl, a cough syrup, to help me sleep; I thought that was ludicrous! We also could not tell anyone what exactly was wrong and what we were seeking help for. None of us really knew. I have been told that I act so normal that no one is able to recognise the urgency of the situation and the need to take firefighting measures, until it is a raging inferno.

That morning I was already 'flying,' to use a young friend's description of this state of mind; I had listened to Simon and Garfunkel's (S&G) Concert in Central Park all night; an album I had great affinity to, as my plane landed in JFK the evening they were playing this live. I had spent a week in New York City, to acclimatise to the US, staying on E 79th Street. Much of this acclimatisation was to hang my sight and half my body from a walkway bridge over a busy highway and ride the waves of psychedelic headlights rushing under me, to get a giddy high. I now put my ear close to the speaker and listened intently to the many variations in sound I could not hear normally and sang alongside in perfect harmony. Mariam and Roby kept vigil and took turns to watch over me in helpless fascination. When *Apia* walked in through the front door I was still crouching near the speaker and S&G were still playing. The skin around my eyes was taut from lack of sleep and my voice was hoarse and raspy from continuous singing. I was not surprised to see *Apia* there, almost as though I was expecting her. I threw on a light jacket and walked with her down the road in the freezing temperature to a small bar that served warm apple cider stirred with a cinnamon stick. I think *Apia* was pleased at being included this way; being so much older than us, she was usually left out. With the warm liquid inside me I ran through the snow, unerringly finding my way to the clinic we had visited in the past days; I, who had such a hopeless sense of direction under normal circumstances. I was inadequately dressed for that bitterly cold winter's day. We went to the university clinic so *Apia* could get advice from them about psychiatric hospitalisation, but I was unaware of this, unconcerned with my plight, unafraid.

The ride to the hospital in Roby's car that night is etched in my mind and I remember with uncanny clarity every small detail of arriving at the hospital to be admitted. My mind did not think to ask where we were going, did not wonder at finding myself in a hospital and there was also no thought of illness. There were several tests carried out and then *Apia*, Mariam and Roby completed the admittance formalities and went home; I do remember the momentary feeling of being abandoned, but it passed quickly. I also did not get any dinner that evening. The room assigned to me was a double occupancy room in which there was no second occupant, and I kept losing my way in the hospital corridors and ending up in this guy's room, who wanted to know if I was a pusher and had any stuff. Since I did not have the stuff he wanted, he lost interest in me, until I wound my way to his room again. I registered the fact that there were so many crazy people in one place and wondered aloud at this. (I remember clearly that I made absolutely no connection on that day with my earlier hospitalisation, five years ago. One reason could be that then we were in a room away from the main ward and I had met no other psychiatric patients during my stay at the hospital in Delhi.) I also have this strange image in my mind that while wandering the hospital corridors my back would not stay straight and my spine started curving back in an inverted U, so I could not walk. The crazy guy had to help me to my bed several times, where I would not stay. Finally the hospital security was called and they 'helped' me to the isolation area, where I spent the night in a padded room. I started my period there late that night, which stained the padding and the sheets, and thought I had ruptured something inside me. (Again, something I only later connected as having experienced at the start of my first episode as well. The next two major episodes happened during my menopause years and this suggests to me that perhaps there is a hormonal connection to these very textbook episodes.) The doctors gave me an injection to help me sleep that night and my mind was in a drunken swirl as sleep finally came. The next morning I found I was still in the isolation area which held very acute patients, many heavily sedated, behind heavy, steel, locked doors and I was not allowed to go to the other side. I stayed there for a few days and was put on medication I knew nothing about. Very slowly I began to come down. During this time I was allowed to meet no one other than the inmates of that special section of the ward...

There is a lot more that I can remember; feelings, fears, sounds, smells, a cold sweat trickling down my back as I talked to *Apia* on the phone and she told me things about my earlier episode that I did not know, things that are now firmly embedded in my memory, but that won't recede to become the memory of a memory, things that I can only experience with my mind and in my soul but I am not, even now, able to translate into words.

They allowed me a telephone call every day and I called *Apia*. I wanted to know what was happening to me and how it was connected to what had happened five years ago in Aligarh and Delhi. She explained a little about the diagnosis made at that time and the change in diagnosis now, explanations of complicated diagnostic matters she had been told that I was in no position to comprehend just yet. I have since come to understand that my extensive 'PhD thesis' written out on Nick's typewriter, on that long scroll of paper, mildly delusional, completely irrational, and which made no point whatsoever, was indicative that I was manic. The doctor there further explained to *Apia* and then to me later, that since I had had an intervening period of normalcy between my two episodes, wherein I was able to pursue higher studies, it did not indicate that I was, in any way, schizophrenic or schizoid; which was the earlier diagnosis in Delhi; in that the symptoms are relentless and there is no reprieve. I was not sure whether I should be pleased or distressed.

Apia also explained to me a little about the treatment five years ago in Delhi and the one part I was curious about, and that frightened me no end, were the four or five Electroconvulsive therapies. I had known through a haze that as part of my treatment I had walked into a room heavy with equipment, which was not an operation theatre, and the doctors had given me an intravenous injection to make me go to sleep. I did not, however, know what it was they did in that room. Kamran went with me and brought me back to my room, and I still don't know if even he knew what they did to me there. Later when I went back to the hospital as an outpatient, the doctor attending to me would often ask *Amma* if I had suffered any memory loss. No reference was made to the treatment. I had suffered no loss of memory and, when there appeared no danger of this, he too stopped talking of it. No one talked about it and as the years went by I too stopped thinking about it, so often. But I never forgot it.

These were all the pieces of a jigsaw puzzle that started coming together bit by bit, to form an unfocused picture. In the US the treatment for a manic episode was quite different in nature from what I had experienced before as an affective schizoid, and it felt different too. The effect of tranquilisers and antipsychotics is far more painful and terrifying than that of mood stabilisers, which are used for the class of illness called manic-depressive bipolar disorder. This illness is not completely destructive as the schizo class of illnesses are and I have read it described somewhere as the artist's illness. Yet some aspects of it and many symptoms are similar to schizoaffective disorder. The medication given to me was Lithium, an electrolyte, which is a mood stabiliser and a classic treatment for manic depression. I assumed the drug was relatively new, but I read that it is one of the oldest in the book. It found use in psychiatry as far back as the mid-19th century, but was formally introduced as a drug of choice for bipolar and unipolar affective disorders only in the mid-20th century. It was almost 1970 when Lithium found widespread use as a treatment of acute symptoms, as well as a prophylactic drug for mania and depression, in the US. It was 1978 when I had my first episode. Is it possible that Lithium therapy was not a part of the doctors' treatment repertoire in the government hospital in Delhi? Or was I not given Lithium because I was incorrectly diagnosed?

Lithium comes in the form of a salt, much like our eating salt, which is a Sodium salt. The Lithium and Sodium salts are what are called electrolytes, which means that when these meet water they split into electrically charged particles called ions. Before the doctor started me on Lithium, I was worried and anxious about the nature of the treatment I was going to be given; having just discovered from *Apia* what an ECT, or a shock treatment as we knew it, was. I also met two older ladies, in their 50s, who were not responding to any chemical treatment for whatever mental illness they had and had to go for repeated ECTs. That really alarmed me and I asked the doctor several times if the same would happen to me. He reassured me, perhaps by saying that Lithium would do the job for me instead. I used to visualise it by looking on Lithium as giving me small, continuous electrical shocks in place of the big shock an ECT would give, something like being connected to a lithium ion battery. It was my own model of how Lithium worked in my brain and has no basis in science, but it helped me believe it was doing its job and I would not need ECT.

At that time my Chemistry professor, whom I always regarded as a mentor, came to visit me often and would bring us a sandwich each so we could 'have lunch together'. She would also bring me a single flower of an intense yellow colour that she would put in a glass of water by my bedside. In her gentle way she would hold my hands in hers and explain to me, "Sara, you have what is called a chemical imbalance in the brain, which mars the communication in and out of your brain, producing all these strange thoughts. Much like the chemical imbalance of insulin, which causes diabetes. As people do, who have diabetes, you just have to eat medicines that stabilise this imbalance, and all will be well." *Apia* tells me that this is the classic analogy given in the medical world and she too gave me the same analogy, to set my mind at rest. More than 30 years have passed since these conversations, but the explanation has lost none of its clarity and it has helped me many times since to eat these seemingly meaningless medicines, despite which my mind keeps losing control of itself.

In the last five years or so, I have also developed diabetes and the explanation was that it is the side effect of the high doses of a particular antipsychotic drug, Olanzapine. I was given, and I went off the drug, to my detriment. Just recently I spoke to someone doing a counselling course, as part of which she attended a workshop with some psychiatrists. According to one psychiatrist, people with my medical issues, which I take to mean bipolar disorder due to a chemical imbalance, may also be predisposed to developing diabetes alongside, and it may not just be the side effect of drugs, as we have all presumed.

By and by I came down from the high manic horse. The crazy, tall man, who thought I was a pusher, was not there anymore and they would not tell me where he had gone. There was another patient, a very quiet, gentle, slow person with a slight hunch and a body that had gained weight rather quickly. I had just discovered coffee with non-dairy creamer and lots of sugar as my drink and we used to meet at the coffee machine, where I don't remember her drinking anything. We tentatively started chatting and she told me the nurses called me 'specky' on account of the large spectacles I wore. I found it funny that the nurses should speak of me. She said she was from a small, neighbouring Illinois town and had come here for the big hospital, and I told her I was from faraway India and would be going back soon (my first admission, even to myself, that I would not stay in the US much longer). I do not know if it was the psychiatric ward culture that patients talk about their illnesses among themselves, as I never did to anyone, other than this one time when this girl asked me very hesitantly what I had. When I said I had been told I had manic depression, her rather plain face lit up with the most wonderful joy for me and she said, "Oh, how lucky for you Sara, only the most creative people have manic depression. I only have thyroid problems," I did think it rather strange that someone was congratulating me on having a certain type of illness. You must remember, this was before the time of internet and email and blogs, and we did not have quick access to information. As I start to read Touched with Fire by Kay Jamison, I am beginning to appreciate what this girl was saying. There is a certain romance associated with manic depression and I sometimes wonder how accurate that is. Even now, well into my 50s, I am told how gifted and talented I am. When I peek into my *jholi,* my bag of fate, I find overriding pain. But when I look more closely, I do now find evidence of that, which is not all adversity.

I have often thought about affective schizoid (or schizoaffective disorder) versus manic-depressive illness (bipolar disorder) as the diagnoses of the first and second episodes respectively, and have explored the comparison after a recent mixed hypomanic episode as well.

I had 23 years of reprieve after my second episode, when I had no perceptible manic or depressive episodes, consulted no psychiatrist, took no medications. I have looked at myself closely during the years when there were no manic episodes, the 23 years of relative 'normalcy' without psychiatric intervention. While it is true that when compared to the acute phases of mania and depression, these periods do seem 'normal,' but when looked at closely, these are not states of euthymia or baseline normalcy exhibited by normal people without this mental disorder. The interim period has elevated states of hypomania, sometimes coming close to mania but not quite, whereas other times harnessed into elevated states of anger or even creativity. When I had this discussion with my doctor recently, and then spoke to *Apia* about it, she said two things in quick succession that were somewhat contradictory – she said the American doctor based his diagnosis of manic depression on the intervening period of normalcy between the first and the second episodes; but then followed it by saying in almost the same breath that my emotions have never really been quite normal after the first episode and other than during the accompanying post-manic depressions, I always remain in an intense, hypomanic state.

I was discharged from the hospital with the categorical advice that I must stay on Lithium for life.

I don't quite remember what happened immediately after that second episode. All I recall is the conviction that I had to go back to India and if I did, I would be well again. I did come back to India after a few weeks, went home to be with *Amma* and Kamran, and then the three of us, she, Kamran and I, moved to Jamia University, Delhi, to make a life of quiet routine in the outhouse cottage in the grounds of a large bungalow. The cottage was a 20' x 20' square, and which was particularly devoid of any architectural pretensions, something a child would draw when asked to draw the plan of a house. Kamran travelled across Delhi to IIT and *Amma* took up a visiting professorship in the Education Department at Jamia; I took admission in the BEd course there. Adil was a frequent and welcome visitor. As the year 1984, which had had such a traumatic beginning, came to a close in this idyllic setting, Adil and I decided to get married. The day I took the train from Aligarh to Delhi was the day I 'chose' my emotions very carefully, hand picked them clean like you would *daal,* lentils, discarded all the uncertainties and became 100 percent sure. I could not have lived with myself otherwise, even if I had brought myself to live with him.

Adil wanted to formally ask *Amma* for my hand in marriage and he came dressed in his best trousers, the brown YSL jacket and a beautiful red woven tie. The idea was that seeing him out of his tattered, unwashed jeans *Amma* would ask what the occasion was and he would pop the question. My contrary *Amma* refused to notice his attire and wanted to talk only about his beard! "Do you think it is like a smuggler's beard or a philosopher's beard?" It turned out to be one of the happiest days of her life.

There was no depression in the weeks and months following this episode; only a very slight slowing down in the initial months of returning to India. Lithium was quite kind to me, and gentle on my mind. It neither elevated my mood nor caused depression. Was this euthymia? I am not sure. I was in touch with my Educational Psychology professor in the US and was making a pretence of reading various books and articles at his request. Some of these *Amma* read too and took notes in her fine, rounded handwriting. She tried to discuss these with me, but I was not interested. I was not interested in anything really. Essentially I was bored, especially when compared to the days just preceding my episode that seemed so exhilarating. Yet I did not want to go back to the US, not because I was afraid but because it had no meaning for me anymore. I again think back to *Abba's* philosophy that you heal when you are bored. *Amma* never tried to relieve this boredom and I simply lay around vegetating. The only decision causing me stress was whether I should return to the US and complete my degree, or not. Once it was decided that I won't, I was at peace. The boredom emptied my mind of all the poison and by the time we moved to Jamia I was ready, with a fresh mind, to begin anew.

Within a year would begin my 23-year remission period.

Almost a reprieve

If you could only see me
And know exactly who I am
You wouldn't want to be me
Oh I can assure you of that

I wish someone would find me
And help me gain control
Before I lose my reason
And my soul

Crosby, Stills, Nash and Young

When I came back from the US, not sure of who I was or how I was, Adil met me in Delhi. This was 1984 and Adil had decided he was going to marry me, although I had not. This time the illness had not ended in abject misery or the same feeling of wretchedness as after the traumatic events in Delhi five years earlier, and that may well have given Adil hope and have something to do with his single-minded resolve. Strangely enough, I don't think so; given half a chance he would have married me in the sun drenched, chilly courtyard of my mother's house when I looked like the elephant man; if only I were able to say just the one word, "Yes." We did get married and I was a June bride in the summer of 1985.

I met many of Adil's friends, strewn all over the world. I used to wonder how someone could have 82 best friends; but that is the way Adil was and has been always; until very recently, when he still has many friends but not in quite the same way. He has had to address crisis after crisis, and other than a very few people, not many understand. I note, though, that Ghazal has many friends the way Adil used to.

It was a very difficult time for me, as I could not bring myself to tell anyone of my affliction. Even if I wanted to, I did not know what to tell. Even if I did try telling, most would not understand. Even Adil did not fully understand what the implications were and I waited every day in dread for the next episode to strike and take us unawares, to shatter every modicum of happiness we had stored away. There was a lot to adjust to, so many people to relate to, a new family to adapt to, and the strain of it sent me into withdrawal, a sort of depression. Other than *Amma* and her brother, no one really knew the extent of my fears, threatening to immobilise all thought. I had no idea where I was headed or what I was going to do with my life. I had had to drop my PhD and come back home from the US, and although I had successfully done a BEd course in Delhi, was even awarded a gold medal for standing first; which I gave to Rumi when he graduated high school and for which *Abba* would have given me one *rupee;* active teaching was still beyond the realm of my capabilities. At this time I also discovered that it was not wise for me to conceive. I was being treated with Lithium, a strong electrolyte, and this carried significant risk for pregnancy. The hormonal changes during pregnancy and childbirth might also make me manic. Faced with such odds, I decided on an MTP, a medical termination of pregnancy, and my child could not be born.

Today when I look back, it is hard, even for me, to assess the extent of my despondency, the smallness of my being, how tentative I was in relating with others, how hopeless the future looked; that is because it was still nothing compared to the year of dark dread after my first episode. In D 84 and M 55 I started stealing alcohol from bottles kept for occasional parties; whiskey, gin, rum; anything I could lay my hands on. While everyone else drank from glasses in a civilised manner, mingling and talking all the while, I drank straight from the bottle, like a philistine, sometimes hiding in the bathroom so no one would know, hiding my shame and tears. No one knew, but I knew; knew the amazing effect it had on my morale, knew how it lifted my spirits, knew how it made me momentarily whole and civilised again so I could go back to the mingling milieu and hold my own, how it created the illusion of greater self worth so I could relate to others. What I did not know, but very soon found out, is that after lifting me up it would crash me down with a diabolical force, a savage fierceness, further down into the dark dungeon of despair; and the cycle would repeat. I am grateful I could get a handle on the situation before it could make a slave of me, the way it has several others I know.

It was just a few months earlier that Adil and I went to his friend's house in Defence Colony (Def Col), a friend who I had not met until then, and we helped ourselves liberally to his homemade orange wine. Quite drunk, I went for a job interview with a carpet seller from Miami and so convinced him of my capability to sell carpets that he offered me the job if I would learn how to drive. Adil sat outside on the curb. When I came out he said, "You are mad," and we rolled home laughing. That was all right, it was just a bit of fun; but what happened later was not; that was what Stephen Fry calls 'self-medication'. Now I truly appreciate my liquor; when I get the chance I drink tall glasses of gin and tonic, with plenty of salt on the rim of the glass, with a very special young friend; with Adil I share a bottle of good wine and with Rumi, an occasional pitcher of beer. And I never drink when I am down.

At this time a friend introduced us to a brilliant psychiatrist and neurologist, Dr N. Now they say he was not such a brilliant psychiatrist after all and that he slipped in later years. Perhaps that was so, I don't know; but for me he was brilliant, humane and warmhearted. He placed his fingers on my psychic pulse and wordlessly promised me that all would be well again; all I had to do was believe that. Our first few sessions, with *Amma* and Adil sitting outside, were spent in silence; the doctor would break this silence to ask me if I wanted to tell him something and I would shake my head. Yet the silence was never hostile, as it was wont to be with other members of the psychiatric community, nor even so awkward. When he recognised that I did not want to talk, but would listen, Dr N talked to me, mostly of Urdu poetry of which he had an impressive understanding, and sometimes of his philosophy of life. Slowly the silence diluted and I began to share my hopes and aspirations with him, but not the unnatural state of my mind and emotions. He surmised what he could from the little I said and drew his own diagnostic inferences. He upped my dose of Lithium and added a mild dose of an antidepressant, the only time in my life I have allowed someone to prescribe me the latter. He is the one who cautioned me: that prescribing too much antidepressant to a manic-depressive patient is inviting trouble. While it does pick you up, it does not know to stop in the normal zone; in a person with manic depression there is a zone above the normal, and this antidepressant may well throw you into this manic zone. A higher dose of a mood stabiliser was needed to keep that in check.

Two months later Adil was to go on an assignment to Singapore for four months, and was not ready to take me along, which frightened me and made me desperate, pushing me deeper into depression. We went for a meeting with Dr N and this time I sat outside, while Adil went in for a long discussion with him. I do not know what was spoken, but a lasting friendship was forged in those hours, and from the doctor's office we went straight to the travel agent to buy my ticket. I can imagine how difficult it must have been for Adil, not knowing my illness and yet having to take responsibility for it. In my moments of misery I used to lash out at him, to hurt him as I was hurting. He reacted and frequently wanted to shut me out.

Dr N taught me how to gauge my condition, wean myself off the antidepressant and then lower the dose of Lithium. The only thing I don't remember too much of is testing for Lithium levels, as Lithium turns toxic at higher levels. Many years later, the chief psychiatric nurse at a Swedish hospital commented that perhaps they do things differently in India, but in Sweden they were required to draw blood to check for Lithium levels. I was resisting this as I have very narrow blood vessels and it is a real struggle to draw blood.

My doctor friend also lent me several books to study in Singapore, which would mirror my condition and help me reflect on it, all of which I did methodically. The books were mainly on anxiety and depression, with just cursory mentions of mania, in passing. I took meticulous notes and organised my thinking. That was the beginning of an understanding of my mind and emotions, an understanding that is reflected in these pages and which saved me from the travails of this illness for the next 23 years.

That trip to Singapore was for me an all-expense paid retreat, where I could steep in the quiet of our 21st storey service apartment overlooking the harbour, and be with myself undisturbed. *Apia* reminds me that she came to visit me there and gave me the diabetes analogy for my illness. Adil had to work long hours and I spent my time discovering myself in the back lanes of the city. For the first time I entered the labyrinths of my mind without fear of the unknown, and what I found was not all dark and murky. I had set up a routine for myself that included strolls down the nearby Arab Street, frequent bus rides to Chinatown or Orchard Road, many hours spent at the National Library. I met someone who introduced me to the world of physically and psychologically impaired children; I spent some time with this little girl who had to be strapped to her chair to keep her head back, but who could still smile. Those four months that culminated in a two week trip to Seoul, taught me a lot about myself, and about me in relation with others.

Upon my return, Dr N finally tapered off the Lithium as his final gesture of faith in me, recognising my ability to handle my illness. I got a job teaching middle school Science and high school Chemistry. I looked after the Science Activity Centre (SAC) of this school and created activities to titillate young minds; a dream come true, the dream I had dreamt in America in my Education and Psychology courses. SAC was a jewel in the school's ideological crown and for me it was a rare privilege to be the one setting it.

Soon after that Azad was born. Adil and I were held spellbound by this miniature person, so perfect in every detail. I was quite sick during my nine months and read many books on childbirth. Adil would say to me, "You're not the first woman giving birth," especially when I tried to involve him in my research and preparation. But for me I was; I had to not only take care of my child, but myself as well. I waited for the hormonal upheaval, and it came, the postnatal blues I so dreaded. I used all my might and mien to fight this and squash it so it would not become psychotic. It didn't. When Azad was three months old we returned to Singapore. I cannot describe the sense of freedom I had, the feeling of breaking loose, of not being defensive about myself, of feeling safe in this protective, yet restrictive, and overly clinical country; and most of all, not having to pretend sanity so as to make it easier for others to accept me. No one knew me and I could make new friends who did not need to know that I was ill, who still don't know how ill I really am, but it would not matter now if they did.

My first eruption came on board a KLM flight travelling from Singapore to Delhi. I was coming home with Azad, who was 11 months old. Barely a day before our flight he had come down with gastroenteritis and was travelling with a high fever, diarrhoea and vomiting; I explained all this to the flight attendants when we boarded the flight and they were most kind, making us as comfortable as possible. Just as the plane was about to pull back they announced that there was a technical problem with the aircraft, we should remain in our seats and they would serve drinks. There was immediate excitement and then mayhem, as my countrymen wanted their booze. I was in the aisle seat with Azad in my lap and the two men, sitting in the middle and window seats, leaned across us, knocking and brushing against my child, reaching out to tap the stewardess on the arm, or even her bottom, in their eagerness to get their shot of whiskey, gin or rum, or all three together. Azad was screaming till he was red in the face and a rash started creeping up his neck. At this point one of the stewardesses turned around and said, "Shush!" to him. She may have wanted to shush the two men, but she took it out on my wailing child. I saw red. I picked up Azad and got up from my seat, pushed the stewardess and the service trolley to free my way and walked to the exit. Everyone asked me to go back to my seat and when I did not listen, they called the pilot. He very politely said, "Madam, you have to go back to your seat," and I started shouting, "Have to? I 'have' to do nothing! I am absolutely not going to go back to my seat and I would like to see you make me. My child is ill and I am not going to sit with him in that sordid tavern you are running in there."

The pilot was taken aback. At this time they asked everyone to deplane as this was going to take several hours. We were to stay in the boarding area where dinner was served to us. The stewardess came and apologised, but something she said seemed to suggest that an ordinary drinks service turned ugly because of the despicable behaviour of the men in that section of the cabin. I was shamed, as every single one of the men in that section of the aircraft was Indian. The KLM staff was superb; they called a doctor to see Azad and gave us three business class seats, one each for Azad and me, and one for the nappy bag!

The first years I just watched Azad grow and change, a habit that continues until today. I bathed him, clothed him, nursed him, sang him a lullaby and my day passed effortlessly. When he was slightly older I talked to him and he talked to me, I read to him, played with him, strolled with him down our street, told him stories and listened carefully to the stories he told me. Four years passed in this way. Then I decided to go back to teaching. I was accepted as a good teacher by the international school community and taught Science and Mathematics. I learnt to facilitate the learning of Mathematics through an individualised programme, rather than teach it to a whole class. It was truly inspirational to watch a child work her way up the conceptual ladder at her own pace and build from strength to strength. I have never since stood in front of a class and taught Maths. We lived in old, colonial bungalows where Ghazal and Rumi were born, and they came like breaths of fresh air. We lived a good life in Singapore and this continued when we returned to India ten years later. I almost began to forget that I had an illness latent inside me.

However, some things would not really let me forget. Even during these relatively peaceful years there was evidence of dips in emotions and small, but sustained, plateaus of mental and emotional storms occasionally, or instantaneous peaks of emotional upheaval that died down quite quickly. Ghazal was born without a ripple, but Rumi came on a huge wave. The postnatal depression lasted for months and became agitation and anger. Rumi was born just when summer started and at the end of summer I decided to go back to teaching as a means of getting over the irritability and lowness. That was a mistake. *Amma* came, we hired live-in help, and I went back to work when Rumi was not yet three months old. As I was still nursing him, I used to express milk for him at work, in the lunch hour, and then freeze it in small Gerber food jars saved from when Ghazal was little. The house help used to defrost it and give it to *Amma* to feed Rumi. It was when I discovered that she was randomly defrosting and refreezing the milk that I lost it. The shit hit the proverbial fan. I was livid and filled with a bilious rage. Rumi got an upset stomach and a severe case of nappy rash. I didn't know what to do, as I still had two weeks of term left. I took the girl off all baby duties and these were left for *Amma* to do, while she did other household work. I became exacting and demanding. If there was even a slight wrinkle noticeable in the clothes she had ironed, I would have her iron them again; she had to endlessly vacuum and mop and wash the bathrooms and clean the kitchen. Then I became paranoid that she was stealing from us and trying to harm Rumi. Fortunately Adil used to cook, otherwise I would have been convinced that she was poisoning us. I used to hide and watch her, though *Amma* assured me that she did not go near Rumi or the food, and the missing things would probably turn up; as they surely did. My fears were not allayed and I just wanted her to leave. The two weeks of nightmare somehow passed and I resigned from the school; they were very considerate. The girl could not take my aggression anymore and left. The agency asked us if we wanted another maid and I declined. The tensions magically lifted and in the calm that returned to the house and my mind, I could cosily cuddle with Rumi and *Amma* and be at peace.

When my mind is troubled, as it obviously was at that time, it starts to traverse back and forth, at sometimes enormous speed, along familiar paths, seeking solace and learning from things overlooked in the past. This accelerated mental activity is a balm to emotional ravages and in that sense, something positive, if moderated. If it remains unchecked it can hurtle past uncontrolled, the anger and anxiety distorting all creativity and shattering all constructive thought. I learnt this when I was a young mother, learnt to pace myself and live for a long while in a quiet moment. Krishnamurti calls it 'staying' with a question; I stayed with many questions all the while our children were young and Adil learnt to do the same. There were always quick answers to be found, but we did not always seek them.

Everyone says I was well during these years, and I say that too, as these years were by and large serene, and are peppered with a creative genius of sorts in many areas. Yet, this creativity is cushioned by hypomania, a kind of continuous mania that does not go through the roof, and its lateral thinking can be harnessed to become productive; as opposed to a full blown manic attack which can only be destructive. Flights of fancy became the basis for inspiration and were not some kind of wild fantasy, whereas delusions of grandeur translated into an assertive confidence. The way I remember my father. This hypomania did not need any sort of medical intervention, or at least I decided so, and I was free of medicines all those years. I was doing something all the time, some of it good and valuable, and that in my context is being well.

The one big example of my hypomanic hyperactivity is the whole conception and creation of Woodsong. My *Amma* died in the summer of 1999, making real my biggest fears. She was my main sustenance, she knew every aspect of my illness, knew what to watch out for and I knew that if things were not right she would be able to recognise this and help me. Over many years she could caution me whenever she felt my emotions were peaking one way or another, when I was too exacting of my children, or my colleagues, or Adil; when my mental activity would forge ahead to the neglect of all else, when I was in pain and it looked to others as though I was high. More often than not, she would instinctively know the inevitable negative truth that looked like something positive to others and even to me. In the beginning I took this for granted and automatically turned to her for help, but never advice. I wanted her to fix things, as Rumi said to me many years later, but not tell me how to do it for myself. Then, while we were in Singapore and Azad was a little boy, her brother, who lived in Delhi, died. This uncle had given me my mind back after my first episode and taught me how to read again; *Amma* and my shared grief, long distance, was one of the most arduous emotions I have had to endure since my father's death. Plus she was not by my side to gently mend matters, so they hurt less. It is then that I began to realise that she was not always going to be there by my side, maybe not even there to talk to me on the phone, even though we hardly did that. In fact she said something to that effect. Some time afterwards I began to practice losing her, practising thoughts and emotions that would render this eventuality bearable in some small measure. I started practising hypomania so that whenever I was under emotional stress I would quit whatever caused it and maniacally get into something else. When she died and was laid to rest in the hot sands of coastal Kerala, I could live my emotions exactly as I had schooled them to be and intense hypomania became my reality then and in all times of affective disturbance ever since.

Kamran and I went to Aligarh to pack up Mishkat and say goodbye forever. I brought back a treasure trove of letters, papers, writings and photographs. Among them were four pages of, what looked like the beginning of *Amma's* would-be memoirs, written in beautiful calligraphic Urdu. She wrote this in 1986, after my first two mental episodes and a year after I was married. My illness that she refers to, is my first mental episode and the strange pain she is carrying is because she had lost *Abba* just a few weeks earlier. Zalsun *Bhaiyya* was her brother, my *Mamoon Saheb.* We could find no evidence of anything more having been written. I brought these pages with me and took several years to translate them, with help from *Babajaan,* Adil's father. You see, although most of the Urdu was simple enough to translate, what was hard to bring out was her understated personality so firmly rooted in her values, her gentle approach to a hardline philosophy of life, her courage, her grit in the face of adversity that I have seen.

~

2.4.86

Dil phir tawaf-e-ku-e-malamat ko jaye hai,
Pindar ka sanam-kada viraan kiye huaye

Mirza Ghalib

My heart again goes circling the path of self-condemnation,
As the temple of my pride lies devastated

I saw this *sher*, this couplet, on Zakaul Hasan's diary (Zakaul Hasan was my younger brother). While studying for his BA he met his death in a fatal accident. He went to the Aligarh railway station to bid farewell to a friend. He boarded the train and while alighting from the moving train he fell from the platform and himself left the world forever. This happened in 1944 when, after completing my BA, I was living in Kanpur with *Khala Amma*, maternal aunt.

I have no idea where that diary has gone. I do not even remember what was written inside. Perhaps I did not read it. Maybe I could not bring myself to read it. I cannot remember anything, except for the title, this *sher.*

Just suddenly today I thought I would write down some of my memories, and so I thought of this title, this *sher.* The title is very good, At that time too I had liked it very much and had felt proud of my late brother's sensitive intelligence. However, I understand now, that for my narrative, which I want to write, this title is not appropriate. My heart is not circling the path of self-condemnation; its memories are filled with happiness and give me courage. Instead of devastating the temple of my pride, these memories will help to build my self-esteem.

My intention is to remember, remember those days gone by that make my heart strong and fill it with courage; memories that have taught me to understand that happiness and sadness, trouble and reprieve, are all relative. Much depends on a person's attitude and more specifically, one's attitude towards one's own self. My memories tell me that all days do not remain the same. Troubles come and then they pass, But they have another aspect to them, which is that they make our hearts, our intellects iron strong, but do not turn them to stone; iron when it meets the heat of life can melt, unlike stone that can only shatter when life gives it a beating. (*Amma* used to talk a lot of this difference and I remember her using the word and phrase, *faulaad* and *sang-dil*, ironlike and heart of stone, very often).

Sara was ill, very ill; and I, with a strange pain inside me, was spending my days going back and forth between home and hospital. We did not know if she would ever be well or not. Zalsun *Bhaiyya*, Nannhi, Kamran, Tintin, Dunu were each helping in his or her own way and in any way they could. One day in JNU I went upstairs and lay down. Zalsun *Bhaiyya* climbed the stairs and came upstairs although he should not have climbed stairs. In addition to Sara, he was also worried about me, lest I fall ill. I was lying down quietly and he came and sat beside me and said, "I used to wonder where you have got this grit from. None of us have it. *Abbajan* too did not have it, but *Amma* had a lot of grit. You have got it from her, We never got any of it, but you definitely did." This was the highest praise for me that until then, anyone had bestowed. I do have grit, a lot of it, and I am proud of this characteristic of my personality. That *Amma* had it I was not aware of, until Zalsun *Bhaiyya* mentioned it. But since then I have thought about it and I remembered my childhood. I thought of my childhood often, but not from this perspective. My memories of childhood are mostly taken up by *Dada Miyan*, (paternal grandfather) and Zakaul Hasan, who was two years younger than me. The two of us would be found circling around *Dada Miyan...* in the morning when tea was made we were near his *samovar*, at breakfast sharing the eggs he boiled and sipping his pure, no-milk tea, in the afternoon hours by the river, sitting on a *charpai* under a thatched roof talking to him, or just hearing him talk.

But every time I looked back at *Amma*, I found her silently attending to housework and the organisation of our home. If our cook or *bua,* who we called *aiyya,* was not there, *Amma* would cook the food herself. Whether *aiyya* was there, or not there, at both mealtimes she would sit on a *peerhi*, a low stool, and serve out the food into the serving dishes. *Dada Miyan, Abbajan*, any of the boys who were home, Zakaul Hasan and I would sit on a *takht,* a wooden platform. The food was laid out on a *dastarkhwan*, a white cotton sheet for the purpose, off which we ate. It was required that everyone sat in this way with *Dada Miyan* and ate their meals. However, our *Amma* sat where she was, on the *peerhi,* and ate; and that too after *Dada Miyan* had left the room. She never thought about this matter, nor did we think things could have been otherwise.

At home there was a *chakki,* a hand mill, as well as an *okhli:* like a large mortar and pestle. Two women sat at the *okhli* and with the *moosal* they would grind the grain and dehusk the rice. On the *chakki*, sometimes one woman, other times two, would mill or split the *daals*, the pulse or lentil grains and on the slightly bigger *chakki* they would grind *besan* or chickpea flour. The grain came from the fields and *Amma* had it weighed and filled in earthenware pots. This job was also done by the same women. *Amma* was busy almost entirely the whole day with these chores, but I never heard her complain even once, or get tangled in an argument with the working women.

In our family we were perhaps short of money, meaning ready cash. A*bbajan* would get some *rupees* as a sort of stipend or salary from the landlord, as he was a farmer who farmed the landlord's land. He gave this to *Amma*. With this money *Amma* would buy *ghee*, oil, etc. She would sit on the ground and keep an eye on the seller women as they weighed and measured out their wares. Then she would herself weigh and measure out the ingredients for the cooks to cook each meal. When food was ready she would distribute the food to various members of the household. In those times all homemakers would do these chores, but I have often heard women in my own family nag and complain of 'not enough' in their lives. However, our *Amma* never did this. With her it seemed that whatever she had was all right. And even if it was not all right, one should keep quiet about it.

But it was not that our *Amma* was an *allah miyan ki gaaye*, a simpleton; or that she enjoyed living in misery. Whenever the moment was right she would not pass up the opportunity of asserting the rights of her children and of herself; which I saw less and Zalsun *Bhaiyya* heard and experienced more, because he was older and understood the circumstances better. *Amma* was not inclined to complain of every small ill that befell her. Despite being deprived of many things, she never expressed the actuality of her deprivation and I am privileged with and proud of the knowledge that she never allowed feelings of want or a feeling that we had less, to take root in the minds of her children.

~

As 1999 entered its last quarter, my rather studied hypomania needed an outlet and I found myself wandering South Bangalore, looking for land to build upon, to build a home that would take away this intense pain of losing Amma and one that would have my signature on it. I never thought of it as a tribute to *Amma*, in fact I don't even remember associating this activity with *Amma*. *My* experience tells me now that it really did not have anything to do with *Amma*, just that her death and the accompanying pain was a trigger for intense thoughts and emotions. I just wanted an escape from these thoughts and emotions that I could no longer bear or perhaps I wanted to define a way of thinking that would make me feel better about myself. I ran the length and breadth of the city, clearing documents, meeting farmers, looking at designs and those who architected them, setting a price to everything and moving so fast that few could keep up with me. Adil was very concerned that I was spending all our resources building a house in the back of beyond armpit of the universe, as he then saw Thatguni village. He only came to site twice in the 11 months it took to build it. However, no one saw the mania in all this, no one connected it to the enormous tragedy in my life, except for *Apia*, who visited in March of 2000 when *Mammijan*, Adil's mother, had her knee replacement surgeries, to find I was already putting up walls of my house by sheer dint of a maniacal *junoon*, an ecstatic madness. If I felt someone was not doing his (or her) job, I would just snatch it from them and do it myself, be it battling with government officials or polishing the red oxide floor or making stabilised mud blocks. I fired, more than hired, architects, as I felt they were taking advantage of me for their own gratification, and finally dispensed with them altogether. I have no idea where the energy came from, but I could feel its force as it coursed through my veins, as could others, and it was relentless. It was enormous energy, focussed and carefully balanced, and it put together my house in a short span of 11 months; put it together so beautifully that it does not speak of the mental chaos and emotional anguish it came from. The energy is now embedded in the very mud and mortar of the place, bringing a sense of seamless harmony to this space we call Woodsong. Adil cannot wait to retire there and start his restaurant, which he wants to call The House of Commons, but I think a better name is *Bazm-e-Shorofa*.

There were periods of intense anger before *Amma* passed away and also after the completion of Woodsong, during the time we were living there. This anger was directed at the school where the children were and where I made abortive attempts to teach within the bounds of a revered philosophy that I felt was grossly misinterpreted and misrepresented. It was also directed at others' concept of charity and charitable organisations I was involved with and various other issues of a spurious nature. One of these others was my friend Tehmina. I was ricocheting my negative emotions off her and from being my sounding board she became a punching bag, an opponent. The anger came out in intensely angry writings, which I have destroyed in shame. Once my children found me writing to her, all in capital letters, and they were aghast. Azad explained to me, quite sternly, that it was tantamount to shouting at her. I know that I was shouting at her in anger, but did not know why. There were triggers that became reasons for this anger. This anger was hypomanic, maybe even manic at times. I had partnered with friends in Switzerland to support the heart surgery of a little girl. This was followed by the brain surgery of a little boy, the son of our cleaning woman. There were so many children waiting for medical intervention and the needy patients' fund of the hospital had no money. I started a drive to collect money for the hospital fund, rolled out emails to privileged people, talked about how privileged we were and went hard and fast. One of these emails, which went to our friends in Switzerland, was a lengthy, intense letter that talked of privileges and the lack of them. John felt I was saying they were underprivileged! I was shocked, as it was obvious to me that I was not saying that. I reread this email several times and then asked Adil and Azad to read it. They too agreed with John that the email seemed to suggest that John and Lily had lesser privileges. These might have been delusions of grandeur that I could not perceive. Or it was just a misunderstanding. In an extremely lengthy correspondence, the sentences running long without many punctuation marks, and fusing into each other without taking a breath, you could not distinguish whether I was talking about the privileged or about those not so privileged. Even I could not tell where I was talking of whose privileges. There were no doctors taking care of me then and I was not under any medication. I became evil in my own eyes, and perhaps in the eyes of others. I have sometimes wondered what Adil and the children thought.

In 2005, when Azad and Ghazal were in university abroad, we took an 11-year-old Rumi with us and decided to move to Sweden, to a town west of Stockholm, in their coldest, darkest time of the year. I still remember the feeling in the pit of my stomach as we drove from Arlanda airport under pink clouds, with the sun about to set around 2:30 pm. Everything was enveloped in darkness before we reached our destination. Lamp posts shed pools of light below, some of which was reflected by the snow on the ground, but much captured and swallowed up by the sheer intensity of the darkness around. The glow of the windows was also mirrored in the cold of the snow, bringing out the warmth of a myriad rooms where throbbed thousands of hearts with a life unknown to me. I remember my chest tightening with excitement and a sharp fright, the feeling I experienced during my theatre days as I entered from the wings and faced an audience. As I write this I realise that right from the start I was preparing to play a part in an, as yet, unknown drama.

The disquiet of winter

If my words did glow with the gold of sunshine
And my tunes were played on the harp unstrung
Would you hear my voice come through the music
Would you hold it near as it were your own?

It's a hand-me-down, the thoughts are broken
Perhaps they're better left unsung
I don't know, don't really care
Let there be songs to fill the air

Grateful Dead

The winters and the summers in Sweden were frank in their stance with a breathtaking freshness and beauty and the first year was a revelation of the possibilities of nature. I was teaching in a small school with just a handful of children, of whom one was Rumi. Sometimes together and sometimes on our own, he and I walked home through the back lanes, looking over hedges at various sorts of domestic activity. Then we entered the warmth of Thuregatan 5, lit candles, cooked dinner, drank cups of tea. In winter Adil would build a fire in the fireplace, in summer, one in the barbecue. The dancing flames told me stories that I wrote down. I also wrote poetry after many years.

Rumi is in Sweden today, eight years later, visiting friends. Yesterday I heard him describe a late winter's day in our little town and many of the feelings came rushing back, as in a dream. Today I have realised another thing, that the feelings just before the onset of a pure manic episode are good, they are surreal, like in a dream, but not like in a nightmare. I would have thought I would recognise these feelings, as they had come to me so many times before. The precedents, the basis, the triggers may have been totally different, but the four seasons of my moods when I was a student around 1983 were very similar to the changing seasons of my temperament in 2007, especially when temperatures were low and there was greater darkness around. The stars seemed to hang lower in the sky and street lamps twinkled.

There was also that peculiar fragrance in the air, that smokiness I have written about earlier. To my great astonishment I recognise it as being the same in the late autumn of 1982 in the US and the fragrance I could recall from the early 1960s when I waited in the Canadian winters with *Apia* for a bus. Was this heightened awareness one of the building blocks of my manic depression, in evidence when I was just five?

There is heightened awareness of sound too and Concert in Central Park or *Raag Yaman Kalyaan* include many more intricate sounds than there were before, which I have listened to and played the latter on my sitar, over and over again, with a whole new perspective each time.

Then in 2007 I discovered Ripple, when snowbound in our small Swedish school. I have listened to a lot of Grateful Dead over the years, but never quite in this way, never with this knot in my heart and mind, as though the words came from there. The ripple in my mind resonated with the ripple in the song and neither caused a disturbance as I soundlessly walked the thin line between the real and the surreal, a road between dawn and the dark of night, no simple highway. Ever since then, two people in my life, my colleague and friend Kerri and Adil, have come to dread the times when I listen to music too intently.

Things took a strange turn on my 49th birthday when a friend died and her husband and two boys came to spend a week with us. I have written about that week, the abject pain and the quiet sadness, the recollections, the memory thrown years back and minute details remembered. My thoughts started churning around and I could feel something ominously familiar happening, but could not recognise its importance, its implications.

I went running to them, weeping in fear and misery, hoping my friends' boys would make up for Ghazal and Azad not being there. Somehow I was convinced that Azad would hold me together, as might the older of the two boys. You see, it had been 23 years since my last full blown manic episode, and although I had forgotten nothing, each episode is different and I did not know how to interpret this one. There was also venomous anger and as I later found out, I was headed for a mixed episode that had elements of both mania and depression. I now understand how different this is from a pure manic episode.

I wrote two pieces during that time, 'And the magic tin comes back' and 'it was just a morning for him.' The two pieces are essentially different. The first is steeped in sadness and contains a soft glow of feelings and memories that flow and envelop everything and everyone. This could be seen as the beginning of pure mania, where there is no unhappiness or depression. Conversely, there is even a sense of joy and a celebration of life when mourning a friend. When I mourned the passing of my father so many years ago, I was able to make this quantum leap to transcend pain and grief altogether and enter a state where these did not exist. I wrote much then too, but unfortunately, none of that writing remains. If I recall correctly, those writings contained the ebb and flow of similar gentle emotions, unquestioning of what had happened and without an iota of jarring anger and disbelief.

~

<u>And the magic tin comes back</u>

The week that my friend's family was with us, Sweden showed all its colours, and generated all kinds of emotions. The leaves had turned a riot of orange and yellow and red hues and most were on the ground. We wanted to hold on to the deep red of our Japanese maple for them, but could not. There were days with bright sunshine, days that were grey, and the daylight hours got squeezed between the two ends of the growing night. The wind howled one night and there was a blizzard that brought snow, which actually covered the ground a few inches deep for a few days, with a soft, white blanket. Rain blew in our faces, wet our toes and brought on sneezes. But it also generated a warmth inside, brought on by candle light and reading lamps, reflected in our big plate glass window, imprinted on a brick wall and on the bark of a tree outside. It was a strange week, tinged with sadness, but glowing with hope and tacit feelings, tastes and the sound of music, quiet conversation and laughter, films, photographs and art, and the written word. I reread Saif's story and found new meaning in it.

Midweek Amit was very tired one evening and much of the following day. He had been emailing perpetually, words just pouring out of him at enormous speed: in the kitchen, in the living room, in the bedroom, on any of the four laptops he could lay his hands on. I watched in helpless fascination. That evening he talked to Adil and I withdrew, as I had usurped much of his time and attention until then. But the green light on gmail came on, again and again.

When 24 hours of our precious week together had gone by in this state, I could bear it no longer, and sat him down with a glass of wine. With my thoughts racing and tumbling and tripping over themselves, and with his troubled face making it very difficult to collect the right words together, I began with something that sounds to me, in retrospect, like the following:

"Slow down, Amit. You are trying to look too far and too wide, too soon. You are hurting and confused, yet trying to heal through reason and all sorts of coping mechanisms and plans; trying to heal yourself, as well as many others. You are looking far ahead, trying to ensure that everything is alright many years in the future and for everybody near and far. You are not looking at here and now closely enough. You have to hold your boys real close, and escape into the present. You have to tune into them to the exclusion of everything, and sometimes everyone else. You are not tuned in enough, as tuned in as they are to you and to each other."

I could see that he was very taken aback by my words and they jolted him, I think; even as I hope they did not hurt or sadden him. "Then I am not a good parent," he said. Then, very slowly and thoughtfully, seeming to consider the possibility that he might be wrong in what he was about to say, he added, "I am tuned in to the boys, Sara. I am tuned in to everything they do, say, write, draw, photograph."

I was very angry with myself for having said what I did. All I could do was helplessly grope for adequate words to tell him that he is a good father, the best, the only one, for sons that adore him and hang on to every word he speaks and every nuance of his body language. I reminded him of what Adil had said when he returned from Bangalore, where he was when we got Amit's email with the heartbreaking news. I was making myself a little sick, worrying about Surya and Saif, not knowing how they would be, how they had grown up, how they would cope, now and later. As Adil walked into the house through the rain that evening, he said,"They will be alright. Look who their father is. They could not have a better father than Amit."

Here is to you, then, Amit; to you and to Sofia, an ode, if you will, to what you have given to your children.

I could not find the words that evening. Then, as I vacuum cleaned the house, while Adil took Amit and the boys into Skavsta to begin their journey home, the hum of the vacuum cleaner seemed to quiet my thoughts into a semblance of order, and the web of words began to untangle itself. I am grateful for the ensuing clarity that emerged, though my words still buzz with the hum of the vacuum cleaner. I have long learnt to accept this hum, and I hope you will too.

A long time ago, in Singapore, we did not know Amit and Sofia intimately, though we knew them well, knew them for a long time and spent a lot of this time together. When Azad, Ghazal and Saif were babies, before Surya and Rumi were born; we were cooking, eating, in one house then another, lunch rolling into tea, tea into dinner; chatting on Orchard Road, walking down Serangoon Road; never too serious about things, yet never flippant, quite caring and entirely comfortable.

Today, looking back, I will say it differently. We knew each other in a different time in our lives, in a different place, when everything was more straightforward, more direct; when reasons were sought and found for everything, and rational thought governed all actions. Or so most of us thought. I had stopped looking for reasons a long, long time ago, but everyone else did and I went along, neither accepting nor rejecting this stance.

I admired Sofia very much. Her straightforwardness, her reserve, her open disregard for all things phoney, her honesty; the way she walked away when something did not hold meaning for her, or when she was simply tired or sleepy; our mutual discomfort at large parties that she sometimes did not attend, and I wished I hadn't. Many, many things that I came to know about her as a person.

That summer of 1997, when we were packing our household to move to India, I met her often. At their house she would make the room very dark and cool against the glare of the sun, drawing close the curtains. We talked inside, with Azad in the living room with a book, Saif and Ghazal always somewhere near him and Surya and Rumi, well, somewhere there. Some time later we left the house in Nepal Park and moved into a serviced apartment that had a swimming pool on the top floor, overlooking the rooftops and terraced gardens of expensive penthouses in downtown Singapore. I recall wondering what kinds of lives people lived in those penthouses. I forget what Sofia said, but it was not very complimentary.

She brought Surya and Saif, once or twice, and we went up to the terrace swimming pool. While Azad, Ghazal and Saif swam, we sat with our legs dangling in the baby pool and talked, as Rumi and Surya splashed around. From my reconnaissance trip to Bangalore I had brought back some Krishnamurti, which I was reading in my attempt to understand the philosophy that Azad, Ghazal and I were to live, a way of life I knew Rumi too would enter some time later. Sofia was deep in her study of Buddhism.

I reminded Amit of this time, the quartet of photocopied Buddhas with the painted blue background that hung in their house. I really liked it and she made me one, which stayed with me for a long time, then disintegrated. Saif reminded me of how she used up all the blue paint from his paintbox to do that! I remember the paintbox, with a hole where the blue colour was.

We talked religion, philosophy, psychology. "Deep thoughts," as Adil would say. I don't know how deep they were or even how meaningful, but it does not matter. What matters is that we could talk, without even a trace of abrasive argument or the need to prove a point. To me that is excellence in relatedness. I was able to speak to her of things I have spoken about to very few people in the world, and even fewer have understood. If nothing else, the quiet hum of our voices must have fallen on our children's ears and soothed their thoughts. I would like to think so, much as the quiet hum of the vacuum cleaner soothed mine.

There were other things, many of which I don't remember any more, that made me hold her in high esteem. Such as when she and her mother rose above their deep-rooted vegetarian nature to cook and feed liver to Surya, who had developed severe anaemia. The first time around they called me for help and advice. I had eaten liver before, but this was the first time I chopped and cooked it. The only thing that induced me to do so was the thought that if they were going to do it every day, the least I could do was to do it for them the first time around.

Amit has always been, for both Adil and me, as well as our extended family and friends, the voice of sanity that comes from a sensitive, incisive, critical and unbiased intellect, and cuts through the mayhem and chaos that is our world. Amit is also the clumsy one who makes Adil look good in comparison. Once we were all walking through a basement car park in Singapore, with Ghazal and Saif riding on Adil's and Amit's shoulders. The two fathers were deep in conversation when we heard a sharp 'thunk,' followed by a wail. Amit did not realise that Saif added more than a foot to his height and had walked straight into an overhanging beam. Instead of keeping quiet, he cracked a joke which, try as I will, I cannot recall. Or maybe he didn't, my memory is really fuzzy now, though knowing him, he would have. We, and specially Sofia, had much to say to him about his carelessness, and I remember Adil hung around the sidelines, looking enormously relieved that he was not the focus of all this negative attention.

He and Adil look similar and I have always felt that there is a very deep grain of brotherhood that runs through them, connected as they are by their incredible minds. They both think with their minds, but feel only with their hearts, and never the twain shall meet. They cannot think too clearly when they feel strongly. Maybe because they are this way their older children; Amit's Saif and our Azad and Ghazal, seem to have learnt early to think and feel simultaneously. At least I hope they have, and I hope they will teach this valuable lesson to Surya and Rumi as well.

When Adil called from Bangalore to tell me about Sofia, all I wanted to do was to meet Amit and the boys; see them, talk to them, and reassure myself that they were all right. I cannot talk on the phone and sometimes I have great difficulty writing. We were deeply moved and felt very privileged when Amit said he wanted to bring the boys and come to us. When Adil went to fetch them from Skavsta, I worried a little about what we were going to do with a 14-year-old and a 17-year-old, for a week. Did not know what to plan, had no idea what their interests were; and Azad and Ghazal were not there to take care of them.

I need not have worried. After all, they are Amit and Sofia's sons and that should have told me how they would be. And they were.

Two absolutely charming young men walked in our side door. I just got a glimpse of them before I got enveloped in their father's huge, warm hug. Years just fell away in that one brief moment as our hearts stood still, unable to accept that one terrible truth from which there was no escape for any of us.

When I had a chance to look, I immediately found the baby in Surya's face. He has the same earnest face of the little boy who sat sleepy-eyed on the black sofa in their house in Singapore, as his mother fed him this disgusting goo that was supposedly liver pâté, while we watched. He has the same big eyes that switch off when he is sleepy and take time to switch on when he wakes, and dense, black, curly hair, so springy to the touch. The little Rumi, when he learnt to stand holding the edge of the couch, would watch him quizzically when Surya woke up from his afternoon nap.

The little boy Saif was harder to find in the handsome features of this young man, and it took me many days to come upon him. Maybe because Adil noticed straight away how incredibly like Sofia he looked, while I lost him in Sofia's features.

They slipped into our home and our lives as though they had always known us and we had always known them. They found corners of our house to park their laptops and connected them to the wireless network; asked Adil endless questions on various computer intricacies; chatted and kidded with Rumi; watched films and MASH with him and me, and when no one else obliged, Surya disappeared into the basement to watch Minority Report on his own. He also took the flak for both of us from Adil, for messing up the alignment of the projector when connecting a laptop to it, so he and I could see photographs on the big screen. We ate pasta and pizza, egg curry and fish curry (the latter in a small window of time that Adil went out of town), and when Surya could not cut his pizza properly, Saif set aside his lunch to cut it for him. One night, or in the early hours of the morning, it is hard to tell right now, the two discovered Azad's clickety IBM keyboard and there was much excitement and discussion that I could hear coming from the room. They were awesome, as Rumi would say.

We walked through the woods, Surya leading the way as though he knew exactly where he was going and then following Adil as though Adil would lead him into a magical land. The two brothers and their father looked through the camera lens, seeing different things with the same vision, or the same thing from a different angle. They took innumerable photographs and videos, of shoes and macs, of light seen from darkness and heart shaped leaves against the dark background of a rough bark.

We took the train to the old town in Stockholm, Gamla Stan, with its narrow streets and alleyways, and walked in pouring rain that drenched socks, and winds that inverted our umbrellas. The brothers fought over who would eat the sole chocolate muffin, and somewhere, made up. We squeezed into the tiny pro-Palestinian Jerusalem Kebab place, down a cobbled alleyway and ate kebabs, and drank coffee and hot chocolate. Into the Science Fiction book shop, down to the waterfront with its reflection of a thousand night lights, and back in the train. More photographs and videos, of light reflected in the water, our conversations reflected in the large window of the moving train and street lamps misty in the rain. It squeezed my heart, I longed for Azad and Ghazal, and I thought of Sofia. Here was where I was going to cut school and bring her, leaving the dads to look after the children, just the week before.

It warmed my heart to finally find two young people who were sympathetic to my endless architectural pursuits and who were actually willing to let me talk about it, and wonder of wonders, reciprocate with their own ideas and interest. (*You have no idea, Amit, how my passion for brick and mortar, the play of ceilings, the balance of light and darkness, coolness and warmth, lines of wood and tiles – and I could go on forever – has driven my family completely out of their minds. For years I took photographs: of ironwork and hinges, of dry masonry, of beams and grilles, of the earth and sea – on every holiday, every outing, in people's houses and from books. Azad, Ghazal and Rumi used to finally plead with me to stop, they could not take it any longer, this complete immersion, this obsession. And it was not the only one. There was, and still is, organic living. Rumi once asked me, "Does everything we eat <u>have</u> to be healthy?" Adil wondered, often not voicelessly, where all this was going to take us. And then one day, without us noticing it, he turned around and converted. The rest is history. My three, of course, don't know any other life, and hopefully 'being passionate' is now deeply ingrained in them.*)

Surya took care to see that his father was not cold standing outside, the first afternoon they were with us, and made sure he wore his jacket. Saif took his father's hand in his when he saw him looking sad, feeling low and took his arm on a particularly slippery part of the road through the woods. They are completely heartbreaking in their understated being, in the face of this enormous tragedy in their lives.

Surya is more unreserved and boldly chatty, in a very nice, open way, arguing unreservedly about things he knows little about. "That was not an analogy; no, it wasn't an analogy. He just said, 'for example.' What is an analogy?" But then he gives in to his older brother's superior understanding, deferentially and without reserve, in matters of photography, computers and drawing. The rest is fair game. He drew underwater cities, tunnel-like landing strips for aeroplanes, discussed real estate prices, took pictures of Adil's raid (?) server, read TinTin and Asterix in every corner of the house and designed bookshelves for my library that would allow people to read the title on the spine without twisting their necks. He talked non-stop about this, that and everything, and has introduced me to halfbakery.com, the hothouse of half-baked ideas. He is adorable and pure genius.

Saif is much more reserved, but very affectionate and wants to share – his photographs, his art work, his school, his friends – and then he is like an open book with a lot of feeling packed into few words. There is something very trusting about him and I want to tread carefully, gently.

He brought a cold with him, they both did, which got aggravated by the wet and cold in Västerås. I discussed with them the virtues of my magic neem pill, Trishun; Rumi, of course, immediately warned them of its legendary bitterness and when I told Ghazal on the phone, she said she really must warn people of the risks they are running in arriving at our house with a cold. Surya took refuge behind the fact that he just could not swallow pills and showed me his big, innocent eyes. To Rumi's utter amazement and grudging admiration, and to my absolute delight as I know what it takes to shove it down kids' throats, Saif actually agreed to give the medicine a try. I gave him the pill to hold so I could go and fetch him some water, and before I could stop him, he just popped it in; not realising, as his father did later, that its bitterness is like a religious experience. He almost gagged and as I ran ahead of him to get him some water to drink, I looked back to see if he was okay.

That is when I found Saif's childhood face, a rounder version of his current chiselled features, slightly lowered eyelids and a wide mouth that smiles a lot. I found him again and again, in the thin shivering body after a shower, with a towel around his middle, and another around his shoulders, curled up on the spare bed upstairs to get warm. I looked in when he was asleep, many times, to assure myself that the little Saif was still there. And he was.

I see Amit and Sofia in these children, just as surely as I see Adil and myself in ours. Their looks, the love they carry in their hearts, their sensitivity and sincerity, their intelligence, their sadness and their joy, their tears and their laughter, all these are their inheritance from their parents. Yet I acknowledge with awe and a sense of humbleness, that they themselves are so much more than that which they have inherited. It is a reassuring thought that tells me that they will be alright.

The thought that I could not pin down in words that evening and do not know if I can do justice to even now, is this: these two people, Sofia and Amit, so different from each other, yet so tuned into their children, were the two sides of the parenting coin. Parents are a duality, not a singularity. We fill in different needs in our children, are tuned into different parts. Adil agonises that he cannot get away with a fraction of what I can, without upsetting the cart. What he forgets is that our children give in to him endlessly, for things I could not even dream of asking them to do.

Saif has incredible insight. He wrote to me in an email two days ago, "I feel that I have just been steered extremely well by two remarkable people and that's how I am who I am." It is my earnest belief that Amit has the largeness of being to be these two people all at once, and as he explained to Surya, cover what seems like a gaping hole in their lives with so many warm blankets, the hole ceases to matter so much, even though it never fully goes away.

I work with children and it is my passion and my joy. It has now almost become a habit. I believe that one must continue to 'bring them up,' incessantly and forever, drawing them out and holding them very close, very tight. Until one day something turns around, and then they bring us up. We have to wait for that turning around, and so must Amit; patiently, actively, without hurrying the process. It is now our job, and for me it is our privilege, to help Amit complete this task. So that Surya and Saif, and Amit himself, "recover from their loss" and can once again be secure in "their inheritance of love." (*This is the highest compliment anyone has ever paid me, Amit, and it touches me deeply, though I am not sure I have done anything to deserve such high accolade.)* So the boys soar ahead and attain the heights Sofia must have dreamed for them and transport their very special father to the pinnacle of joy all parents hope for and the fulfilment they aspire to.

Having met the boys now, who carry their parents in their very soul, I know they will.

I am sitting in the classroom and we are working on Maths. They are, and I am writing in the short-lived quiet. A very special student, Jasmin, my favourite, whose dad also works with Adil, looks over my shoulder at the screen, because the Skype button is bouncing up and down for attention and she can relate to that, as she does the same thing, irritating the hell out of everyone. Not for attention, she just does it.

She says, "Boy-oh-boy, Sara, you have a lot of information there, what are you writing?" Our youngest Year 4 student asks," Are you writing about the Magic Tin?" It is an old Threptin tin (Threptin biscuits are vegetarian, high protein biscuits that the elderly eat in India. These we loved pinching from their tins stealthily and eating in hiding. They are like sweet sandpaper that melts in your mouth.), which we fixed with a rubber band and hanging bolt mechanism inside, so when you roll the tin away from you, it reverses at a point and comes back to you.

I say, "No, I am writing about two very special boys and their parents. I am writing about all the things their parents gave them, but how they are so much more than that... complex?" I ask, and Jasmin says thoughtfully," Uh-uh, maybe no." Her year-mate and her voice of conscience and reason (They are the two oldest students of the international class and are quite a pair!) cuts in to tell her to shut up, sit down and do her work.

~

The second was written a few months later as I stood at the brink of a breakdown. We were trying to get Rumi into the dance section of the school to which our international school was attached; firstly, so he could dance and secondly, so he would have some respite from his mother, who was his teacher for everything. The latter was extremely stressful for both Rumi and me; although we were accommodating with each other, this couldn't last and unexpressed anger had begun to build up in both of us. I was relieved when this international school dissolved and Rumi could go attend a proper international school in Stockholm city. Besides, meetings were always in Swedish, which made me feel out of my element.

The thoughts here are disjointed and quite dark, and the words are running ahead of the thoughts, both the thoughts and the words jumping around, speaking to and about different individuals and speaking of different events. It was written largely in pronouns and made tenuous connections without any basis. The 'you' addresses children and young adults I am writing to, my own and others', and the 'she' and 'he' describe many different people I am writing about. It is hard to read and certainly does not make a great read, but I request you read it nonetheless, as it is essentially unedited, except to hide personal identities, and shows what thrashing emotions can do to the flow of thoughts. It has still not lost all coherence as did my 'doctoral thesis' in the US during the episode of 1984 or the 'petition' written on blue paper I mention later, but these I cannot reproduce here as they no longer exist.

A few days later I was in hospital.

~

> *the most extreme expletive is 'heck', and if i say shit*
> *it means trouble. i won't even say what happens*
> *with the rest!*
>
> *i suppose it is trust that gives you the security that*
> *you can just say 'heck' and it will be listened to.*

i sometimes wonder when any of these people will learn how to deal with issues without turning them into a bipolar manic-depressive episode. you are right, they are sometimes so stupid they may as well be illiterate. when will they understand that teachers are very powerful people and can demand total trust and involvement, but in return only sympathise with condescension? when will they understand that it takes a lot of courage to cross boundaries, of nationality, of religion, of relationship? when will they understand that it takes even more courage to make an identity for yourself when you are in a minority, and don't abide by boundaries? when will they understand that others hurt, feel insecure, feel angry?

the meeting was again the usual nonsense, a repeat of the earlier meeting as though that had not happened, as though my letter was never written: 'we have considered your demands carefully and can only offer your son admission in the dance class, but without dance'. no, it was not a demand, it was a discussion you and i had had, where even you considered it important that a child have a total educational experience, and not just be homeschooled by his mum the entire time that he is in school. the language teacher then explained the whole dance contract business, and how these young persons were being groomed to become A class dancers, and this child would always feel at the bottom, feel different and lost. no, i did not ask her whether she thought the dance teacher was stupid and did not have a tongue in her mouth, and yes i know i might have.

in the end his dad and i explained to them the following: to the dance
and language teachers we confirmed that we understood their position,
that they would not be very keen to take in and be comfortable with
a student who starts at the very bottom of their classes, potentials
notwithstanding. to the principal we confirmed that we did understand
the school's position, the structure of these profile classes within the
ground school which provide specialised learning in these areas, and
how the administration did not have much scope. his dad does not really
understand these intricacies, but he was able to say 'i do understand,
but i do not necessarily agree' and i said to myself 'oh god, what is he
getting into?'

then we explained to them how we looked at it, over and above their
difficulties and issues; that we did not see why. why, when a dance
student or any other student, who is at the bottom of the maths class,
and not able to converse two sentences in english, is allowed to study
maths and english with everyone else, a child with no experience in
dance cannot study dance with great dancers. we did not see why his
classmates cannot find him in the english and maths classes, even if
he is a little lost in the dance lesson; because after all, he is only in year
7 and doing year 9 maths and english, and is better at it than they are.
even the year 9 kids could find him there and he could hold his own.

finally i had to say to them that my point, which i made two fridays ago
and was surprised that it was to be discussed in meetings, amongst
teachers, with the principal, is simply non-negotiable, end of story – the
child will not go to the dance class unless he is given the opportunity to
dance, no matter what.

i was not angry, only tired. and frustrated. but not tired enough to not
feel a sense of desperation creep in, with the recognition that these
people were just not going to understand how special this situation
was, how unique the child. he was the only one in the entire school a
different colour, one of very few of a different nationality, the only one

who had his mother attached to him almost 24 hours a day, the only child working several levels above his own in at least two subjects, ... what kind of a recommendation did they want for him?

then the principal began an apology, and i had to cut her off. I suppose that is when i was angry, very, very angry, trying my best to not really control my anger. for a moment i wanted to kick ass. but i did not; i just told her that there was no need to apologise, that we completely understood their position, and hoped they understood ours and the reasons why we were not prepared to negotiate on it; and that it really did not matter.

this part was horrible, and the most difficult for me; it was as though they saw our position, perhaps even agreed with it, but were not willing to take a stand against their own red tape because we were not significant enough. it was then that i had to let my mind fly, take wings to another time, another place. i thought of my father, left to choose between india and pakistan; i thought of my father's talk on bbc, a voice from a long ago past. it was in chaste urdu and we had a lot of difficulty understanding it. the basic thesis, as i have since understood it, was that many indian muslims chose to stay in india. his assumption that the structure of indian politics, that had allowed muslims to remain in india, would by its very nature make a place for them in mainstream life.

my mind flew some more, and i was reminded of 1991, i think it was, just past the kar seva mania, when babri masjid had not been felled still. we came into delhi from singapore and could not go to aligarh as there were widespread riots, not just in aligarh but all around, somewhat like in the 70's, maybe even more. His dad and i had seen the 70's riots, i had lived with the devastation for many years after he left for pilani, after high school; and we did not want to risk it, as we had a child with us. we took the labels off our suitcases so no one would know our last name; our son in any case called us by our first names, although we had started calling each other abbu and ammi to teach him to do so. we knew not to call each other abbu and ammi, and we hung out in delhi and went over to shimla.

there were many high flying parties in delhi during those days, and his dad and i went to one or two. in one, at ks chacha's house, they were watching the india today video on the kar seva frenzy that had taken over the north of india; the same kar sevaks, the hindu militants that babajaan and mammijan, his dad's parents, had encountered on a chhoti line, small rail train station platform, near bareilly i think; on a completely empty platform in the dead of the night, just a short week ago. mammijan was in a sari, and knitting, babajaan was in his harris tweed, reading a newspaper in the dim light, when a bunch of these shouting, dancing demons in saffron robes came onto the platform, high on something, bhang, waving their trishuls, their menacing tridents. the two sat quietly, not talking, not looking at each other, silently praying and thanking their god that they were dressed like modern indians, and there was nothing to give away the fact that they were muslim.

as these people watched their video, these high flying executives, engineers, journalists, advertising guys, much like his dad and i, though i don't remember another school teacher there, they did not look very different to me. they talked and drank and smoked and argued, laughed too, but not one was angry, deeply angry. i was, but i did not open my mouth. his dad was, i suppose, and so were our hosts somewhat. finally they could stand it no more and told his dad 'you can tell them that you are a muslim'. dad just smiled and an awkward silence fell. and then this guy made a mistake, this really suave guy from j walter thompson. he came up to his dad, placed his hand on his elbow and said, 'sorry man. i really didn't mean it like that' ---- he had been saying "these ma dar choot, mother fucking, bloody muslims should just go to pakistan and leave us alone in peace; that harami, that bastard jinnah took pakistan for them. why are they sitting here and making life miserable for us?" ---- 'and besides, you don't even look like that kind of a muslim'. his dad jerked his hand off his elbow and very slowly turned around so he was facing this guy, and then very quietly said, 'till now it did not bother me at all; it still does not bother me what you think, but now you are crossing a line you should not'. we stayed the entire party, and so did that guy, but no one talked about muslims any more.

a year later on 6th dec, a black friday i think it was called though i don't remember too well if it really was a friday, the muslim holy day, babri masjid fell, was torn down and there were widespread riots. if i have my political history right, that year there were no riots in aligarh because it was under bjp rule, but we could still not go to aligarh as it was under precautionary curfew. the curfew lifted for two days and we made a quick visit from delhi where we already were, and discovered the atrocities that were committed in the silence of the curfew, with no one in sight. i met my friend of the 70's who still washed bodies, half of whom were cremated, half buried, randomly, without regard to who was a hindu and who a muslim. or so he said and had been saying for all these years.(he was my theatre buddy, and we went for all our theatre workshops together. he was somewhat younger than me and was my brother's namesake. we went together with his older sister who had my younger sister's name, until the day a truck hit the rickshaw she was riding in and she died. then it was just he and i. he also had an even older sister, not part of this subversive drama club, and she and i shared the same name, sara. this was the strangest coincidence of my entire life. each of our namesakes in their family was older than each of us, their father was a professor in the same university as our parents, and our parents did not name us after them; they did not even know their names. this is perfectly true, however incredible.)

i have often thought that washing bodies was a drama he was playing in his mind; otherwise how could he stand it? year after year, hundreds of bodies. perhaps it was a drama, a bit of histrionics, but i know now that for him it was real, horrifyingly real. i never said anything to him, only listened.

when we came back to delhi, mamoon saheb, my mum's brother, asked me to come sit by him and not turn the lights on. he spoke to me of many things, this gentle man, a patriot, and also the editor of a newspaper in delhi, one who was a wizard with words and helped me a lot when i went through a difficult time, my best friend's dad and my dad's best friend, his dad's fantasy and science fiction buddy, with his shock of white hair. this man who always had difficulty talking, and who thought that the telephone was the worst invention in all the world (and hence probably my aversion to the thing, but i still like to chat with you kid, every which way, even in that box) and would ask me to sometimes just go and disconnect the phone, (why ever was your phone disconnected on saturday, or was it friday, baby?) but not to tell his daughter who got a lot of phone calls (she is an artist in delhi. chand. i told you, this problem with phones is not restricted to your generation :)

this wonderful man who was my dad's confidante, (my dad and he were friends before my mum and dad were married, and they both trusted his discretion in all matters) his room mate all through university, part of the progressive writers' movement, a communist party worker who had been underground and in jail, and had just about seen everything, but could still trust ---- he sat me down in that darkened room and spoke some of the most painful words he had ever said to me in almost 35 years. he said "bibi, i have always been a little upset with you and your husband for not living in india. your mum needs you, and more than anything else, you need this country. i have even tried to convince you to come back. now i must confess though that i have been wrong. it hurts me a lot to say this, but it is true that you have shown a lot of common sense by just going away and staying away. do that for as long as you can, you will pay a very heavy price if you came back; you will regret it and i will never be able to face myself". That was the most that he had ever spoken to me all at once, though we chatted often, he, his son and i, sometimes my mum too. i asked him why, but he would not say. i also asked him if he was angry about something and he said 'yes, i am, i just am'. he never told me a single lie ever.

the day before we left to go back to singapore he talked a lot again, this time sitting out in the sun, in broad daylight, his slight frame wrapped in a shawl much the same way as i wrap a shawl close around my shoulders when i get all cold. i found out how he went back to the newspaper and started working again after he had retired. how the same people who went back almost 50 years with him, who had been through the entire independence movement with him, went to jail with him, had now turned away because he was a muslim; would stop talking in his presence because he was a muslim; but he still went back to work every morning, taking the slow, violating abuse.

i went back to singapore very very angry. I met him a few times after this, and already much had changed in india, and it was apparent. we never spoke about this though; several years later he died, but i never knew whether he changed his mind or not. i don't think he could have

his children have also been very close friends of mine all my life and i met them in delhi when we went to lucknow recently. his son is the one who has been stuck in india for months, not able to go back to the US because DC would not clear him for security reasons. you have to meet him to realise the absurdity of this; leave alone be a terrorist, this silly man could not even swat a fly with a newspaper when my mum asked him to. I don't think he would do any better with a fly swatter.

however unbelievable it may sound, i still trust india has a place for muslims, for me, and this has nothing to do with what i have written above.

i was already switched off and very far away, and a very nonplussed principal bought his dad and me some coffee, and then asked us if we wanted to be by ourselves to talk about it. his dad looked at her as though he did not know what she was talking about, as he had a meeting to go to. and i had exactly 3 minutes to bolt down my coffee and run for a lesson. for those three minutes we grabbed the most 'comfity', as my special student would say, armchairs, drank our coffee and counted our blessings.

there were many blessings to count. it introduced us to a ballet teacher who must have been at least a hundred years old, lined all over her face with fine wrinkles, like that doll in the shankar's dolls museum in delhi, on bahadur shah zafar marg, over which the newspaper office was where my mum's brother worked for so many years and beyond. i saw the doll years ago, but i could still draw it for you if i knew how to´draw. i can't draw, but i have the doll's features etched in my mind.

this lady is a ballet teacher, and my son will learn ballet from her, possibly every monday. she can still tuck in her stomach tight, drop her shoulders, lengthen her neck and become the most beautiful swan. she has an acid tongue and the kindest heart. my little boy did a wonderful job; he was relaxed and happy, dancing and chatting with a partner who must have been about my age, twirling at the bar, sometimes unmindful of what the teacher was saying, just the way he always is, whether it's maths or p.e.

i just watched him for a little while that sunday, when he had the ballet trial lesson, but i did not want to make him feel awkward. so i sat way at the back of the balcony, with my macbook pro and my notebook and pen, and wrote, to strains of the blue danube and swan lake, and even parts of some tchaikovsky and mozart, bits and pieces that i could recognise from the very far reaches of my mind, coming from a little grundig spool player that belonged to my parents and which his dad could not wait to get his hands into every time he visited. when he started visiting me a lot at home he would tell me that it was not because of me that he came, it was because of the grundig player! he fixed it once, and my mum told him she would give it to him. she did, and it lies in the library mezzanine at woodsong. she also said he could have the radio with the tubes, but i could not find it for him at mishkat, the niche in the wall that held a candle.

when his dad came in later, into the balletskolan, we watched our little boy, for the last 10 minutes of the lesson, and felt very proud of him, of his ease, his poise, his grace, and of how natural he was, totally uninhibited, unspoilt. we spoke to the grand ballerina and found out the details: she patted our son on the cheek, explained to him how his body did not seem to listen to him fully right now but would in time, and that he would see a difference in just 3 or 5 lessons, and asked him if he would come back. In reply the may-be ballet artiste just smiled, cocked his head to one side and said 'maybe, i think so' and smiled some more. in the car he looked at his dad and me, and said 'but not on the weekends'. we had a little argument about that as we can only guarantee to drive him just on the weekends, and there may not be a bus there, but we went to the shop in the little red house, and bought black ballet shoes when he wanted white, black leotards, and a t-shirt with a great silver motif, as a bribe:)

this morning he found out that he can go to his ballet lessons with another schoolmate, a very sweet little girl who tells my special student to shut up all the time, who speaks long winded sentences that really tire you, who is having oh, so much difficulty with long division, who can't seem to remember her times tables even with all the memory cards, and now she has to divide with decimals. oh dear, the dot just appears everywhere. i had to make her a cheat sheet on a yellow post-it:

1. does it go in the first number, the first two, the first three........?

2. how many times does it go?

3. make it go, do division.

4. multiply, to check and find the remainder.

5. bring down the next number from top.

6. go back and start at 1 again.

7. if there is a decimal point, place a dot just above it in the answer, and DO NOT put any more dots anywhere else.

hmmmm. i wish that was all. she does not know when to use 'their' or 'there', and sometimes uses 'they're'. her big handsome father who wears cologne and lives in the middle east, thinks she needs to toughen up as she is too chicken; she did not want to go up in a helicopter with him as a pilot, and he shouted at her, but she still did not go. she turned 11 two days before this last christmas. her dog died some months back, he was older than her and was got when her mum and dad were together.

still, she is better at ballet though, and mine will have a lot of catching up to do.

....

i had just gone on gmail (no, meri bachchi, i don't {always} open gmail to write an email in school) to look for some geoboard lessons to do pythagorus with my homeschooled student, as he had chewed up the dime (maths) booklets and had tasted blood. the sweet ballerina kept coming back to me with each step of her division that only involved multiplication up to 5, and the answers were neatly rounded off, and i had to be very, very patient; i had just explained the outcome of the meeting to my son; i had no energy, and there was a long lesson ahead with the 4th and 6th. i looked behind the screen and found the two youngest students playing cards, the only year 4 student and my special year 6 girl.

it was 7 minutes into my lesson. even before i opened my mouth, the sharp year 4 boy saw my look and said 'ok, let's put away the cards' to his friend, and i said 'i should think so'. there was deadly quiet, i heard some playing cards go swishing across the table, i heard someone say 'don't throw the cards', i heard a chair move, and when i looked up there was my special student standing on this side of the screen, just a few feet away from me, fists clenched, eyes big and watery, and she began to shout and cry, 'i don't understand; i just don't understand, why every single time i need to put the cards away; i just don't want to do that, and i don't understand why i should, why i have to, and i just won't. so there.'

i have taught her for a year now, and have seen her upset only once in my presence, when the same friend (again) logged her out without letting her save what she was writing. we had to go up for sewing; she does not like sewing, i don't like sewing and did gardening instead when i was her age. i understand that i have no choice but to teach it, she doesn't. she is just a little girl, a bit of a genius at maths, but still a little girl. (later in the lesson, when the storm had passed and all was quiet, she came close to my ears and said 'sara, i'm going to use the facilities' and smiled :)

but at that time she was really distraught. she sat down on her table in the corner, placed there so she does not get distracted by others and does not distract them, clenched her fists and banged them on the table, put her head down and said again and again, 'no, i don't understand', and without thinking i said 'maybe you should have thought of discussing it 8 minutes ago, as i really want you to get your maths out; you are doing a great job with coordinates'. I so hated myself for saying this and i was trying not to look, though she was right in front of me with her back to me; i heard some banging sounds, and knew that this was going to be difficult to turn around, when she turned and faced me, with anger and fear written large on her face; she had had a full blown nose bleed, all over her face and the table, and she got up and ran.

i know it was only a nose bleed, and kids have them all the time --- last year there was the little boy from UK who had a nose bleed three times a day, and had to bring a spare shirt to school. he was a little like the sweet little ballerina with number operations, only worse ---- i cannot describe what i felt. i knew my special buddy does not use the toilets nearby, and always goes upstairs, another thing she has been in trouble for. heck, i don't use the bathroom here, i go to the other end of the corridor, into the fancy clean ones inside the personnel room. what difference does that make? i ran out and asked the two year 7's to follow her, and thought i would look for the nurse. then decided to look in on her first. the two year 7 students were outside the toilet door, with their mouths to the door calling out her name, and it was absolutely quiet inside, not a sound. i called her too, i told her i was not angry with her, that i was not upset, that i was sorry, that i really wanted her to open the door .... when my son turned to me and said 'ammi, i think i know how to handle this better than you, why don't you go back to class'.

it was frightening. i came and got the two big boys, sent one to look for the head teacher, one to look for the young teacher whose mom teaches here too; he does individual p.e. with this student, to address some special physical needs, and they like each other very much. the teacher is also a part of the school maintenance team and would know how to open the toilet door if it became an emergency. (it turns out that my son figured out how to click open the lock with his locker key, working from outside) and i went in to call -- who? someone, on the phone.

it could not have been more than 30 seconds when one of the boys came back and said she was out of the toilet and the year 7s were talking to her, and that i could go back up if i wanted, or i could .... but i said for us to both stay out of it. by now i was shaking really badly, with cold and fear. what if the child had hurt herself in her anger.

the dilemma is, how is one to deal with this as a responsible adult, without trapping this very special child in continuous exposure, and her own anger and frustration?

the two year 7s and a visibly less angry year 6 child came back soon enough. i asked her to get a drink and come and sit with me on the idrottshallen window, the gym window just outside our classroom. she said she wanted to sit on the left, her favourite side, and i let her, and i sat on the right. for a while i did not know what to say, and we sat quietly as she drank her water. she had put her feet up on the windowsill and i placed my hand on one of her white socked foot, and talked to her for a long long while; she did not say a word, sometimes looked at me, sometimes into the empty gym. i don't know what i really said. something like this

> *'i know things bother you, baby. and then you get very angry. but you need to avoid that, right? you need to keep an eye on the clock, and i cannot let you mess up your maths lessons; you are so brilliant in maths, and i feel very special when i work with you. i felt special when you shouted at me too, but i didn't like it very much; in any case it is such a waste of time. it wasted the year 7s' time and now they are late for their own lesson, it wasted your classmate's time and you know what a hard time she is having with her division. i too would have liked to get my lesson together for 7 and 9. i never push you, i never insist you do what you find difficult or boring'*

on and on and on; and when i said, 'i never ever get angry with you, do i?' a big smile slowly spread across her face and she said, considering each word as she spoke it 'i really don't believe i remember one single time when you have been angry with me, sara' (she is superb in english, swedish and german), and we went back to the lesson.

I know what you mean, about she throwing a lot of tantrums these days and other people getting into trouble or feeling bad because of it, but sometimes there is no choice; we have to take care of her first, as she has some very basic special needs that no one else has. I told her i would not talk to her parents about this, nor will the class speak to her about what happened today, but i had to tell the head teacher as i was required by law to do so. she understood that.

my special student could do a lot of work after that. she went on to 12G in 2R, coordinates, and understood what a y intercept was. i showed her how she could read it straight off the graph, almost instantly, if she felt lazy and did not feel like calculating it; how she could calculate it from a straight line equation and must do so sometimes to stay in practice; and how she must report it as (0,y) pair. She was impressed, and told me that i was quite good, and then just chewed up the whole exercise. She also understood in physics why, in daylight, a white paper looks white, a black paper looks black, and oh, wonder of wonders, why grey looks grey.

I know all this has been said over and over again, but it needs to find new voices to say it, new connections to be made, new hearts and minds to lodge in. there are very special people around, who are in a minority. these minorities may be a religious minority in a country torn with communal violence, and may include a unique individual that lays the dead to rest in order to find peace of mind; it certainly includes those very special students that each of us must strive to be, as only then can we understand them.

i rest my case, and feel an overwhelming sense of weariness.

....

this morning was actually alright. i was rested, and had slept quite soundly. i was relaxed and could do my 'cheat sheet' for you, about the 12 days of christmas. my special student likes the 'insufficient dowry' version, almost to the exclusion of the original. My home school learner spent his entire lesson on it, and wonder of wonders, could actually crack it with just two hints--- right angled triangle and rectangle numbers --- and i could let him see your 'cheat sheet', chanda.

the morning in school was alright too, rather nice really, with few sounds. the older boys showed me the mac os leopard with its time travel, but i was not able to hear its presentation as the school computer does not have a quick time player. it reminded me of the few months old lion cub i held in my arms at the lucknow zoo, and felt it warm and throbbing with life, against my chest. the cub was being acclimatised and was sharing its pen with a deer, very much like the ones that stopped by our garden two nights ago. i thought of gambir, the serious baby elephant; and inuka the polar bear that gave birth, on your birthday, in sweltering singapore.

i let my phone ring for one of the boys, with the aligarh tarana on it, and told him how i had sung it on stage, at convocations, at the sir syed dinner, oh, so many times over.

i also told them a joke from 'a mathematician reads a newspaper'; or is it mr. tomkins who reads the newspaper? I should have left a few more brain cells before lobotomising to this extent.

my special student was alright too, discovering 'sound' on her own in a fairly quiet lesson. she got stuck on one question on 'changing voice pitch', but that was easy; all i had to do was ape your breaking voices! she was awkward in the morning though. when i said hello, she said 'hullo pullo', much the same way you still say 'give me fud', when we have been angry at each other. she felt i had let her down yesterday, but she also knew that she was a big enough girl to let things be. i don't know if she knows that i had no choice, but she doesn't really need to know that, does she?

lunch was good too, but then i walked home. still need to go back as there is another lesson, just with the two youngest students. oh god.

i came back because i was restless, not upset or unhappy, certainly not angry, just restless. at home i walked out the back door and found paw marks in the snow, of the cat from next door that climbs on our garden wall and comes down the slope of the yard cellar roof. there were other paw marks that looked like a dog's and made me wonder. and the fine feathery prints of some bird that had walked up to the back door and walked away. i would have thought it is still too cold for birds here, but early this morning i saw a whole bunch of black coloured birds fly across the sky in perfect formation, going north. just like we saw every evening in aligarh, just like the handful of parakeets that fly over the house at Woodsong. perhaps they are confused about the weather too, like the narcissus that tried to bloom outside a few weeks ago.

i took some pictures, but don't know yet how to transfer them to the laptop. the pictures are safe in the camera. i took pictures of dried twigs too, that had dried over the autumn and winter weeks, reaching out from a mound of snow. i also took a picture of the snow on the ground, which looks a lot like clouds under the sapphire blue sky; but the sky is grey, and i took a picture of that too.

i am still restless, as there is yesterday to reckon with. and i must write.

continually or continuously is the question.

well, is there a tomorrow?

there must be, and so the soapy water in the washing machine must wait to be drained. at least the clothes were washed.

....

i cannot really write much about yesterday, as there isn't very much to say, except that my special student was angry again, and i exploded at the head teacher.

i have thought a lot about it, and i don't know if i am right.

i exploded, not so much at a person, but at issues and concerns i have been feeling for some time now, for several weeks and months.

i feel so did she.

i exploded at a person i had exploded at before, and yet i was deeply mortified.

she exploded at a person at whom she had never exploded; in front of whom she had never exploded, even at someone else, even if she was very very angry about something; in front of whom she has never shouted before; in a lesson that was her only strength, the only place in school where her self-esteem is preserved. In every other lesson, with every other teacher, in every other situation, she explodes all the time, and her parents receive this information via email.

i got a note from her mum, and when she came in to fetch her she was surprised she had hit the 'send' button. the note said that if she is unable to function in class then i should have her call her. that she rarely got ill, but this morning she was so so tired, so very quiet ---- i am glad i got the note.

she proved to me in the last lesson that her confidence in maths is not going anywhere, and even with a bit of a hand-eye coordination issue like you had, she could still draw straight line graphs after solving equations that were not so simple. The graphs were near perfect, and she snapped up the difference between a positive slope and a negative slope almost effortlessly.

i am concerned that she may worry about her self-image in front of me, and that bothers me very much. I don't think so, as she too is a bit of a 'wisdomous' like you, raja, and i do cling to that hope.

> *after the awkward hello this morning she took off her pullover to show me her t-shirt that her grandmother left for her. It had pictures of fish with some writing, and on top it said IQ ALPHABET*

> *"you have plenty of that" i told her.*

> *"sure do" she said with a smile.*

*and then she did the nicest thing. she gave me a
hug that is usually reserved for him. something tells
me that t-shirts are a brilliant form of bribe, and i
must remember that :)*

~

There is relevance of these pieces here; when I read them later and analysed them recently, there are elements in both that point to intense emotional activity. I have traced this same intensity of emotional activity preceding all my manic episodes. In the more recent mixed episodes the intense, pure and surreal emotions get tinged with real anger that pulls me down and renders my emotional state quite ugly, even in my own eyes. Kerri bore the brunt of this ugly side as I pushed her against the wall and did not allow her to get a word in edgeways, to tell me that although this was my reality, she did not understand it. How could she, when I was scaling heights she could not even fathom? On the one hand, I did not care who understood and who did not; on the other, you had no choice but to embrace my deluded reality and become part of it. On the walk home from school that day I lost my way. There was snow piled on the ground and falling heavily from the sky; the whole landscape around was covered in white and obliterated from the face of the earth. There were just undulating mounds of snow and streets were clones of each other. Twice I slipped and fell. My heavy duty UGGs could not hold on to the compacted snow and ice and my balance was tipsy. The second time, I just could not get a foothold to pull myself up. I do remember it crossing my mind that I did not know where I was, but did that matter? Thuregatan was on top of a hill and I was probably circling the top as I could see a highway way below, the silence merging with its deep growl. I had lost the concept of time too and have no idea how long I was floundering in the moonscape. When I finally reached home, Rumi was there already; the candles were lit and he had made a pot of tea. All he said was that I should have taken my usual way home. That night a person from Adil's workplace came home for dinner, an Indian gentleman just moving in and considering our school for his child. Adil cooked the dinner and I remember not letting my anger show against the school. I told Kerri the next morning that I could hear shoes up on the roof, of people spying on us, and they kept misplacing my packet of cigarettes hidden in our bedroom balcony.

I had much to say in anger at first, but then I was not aware that no one was listening to my harp unstrung. Then without a word I stepped into ether, where I did not need to say anything, everyone heard me and everyone talked to me. Even the driver of the taxi did not ask if I was talking to him, but he did not buy me cigarettes either, though I begged him all the way. By then my thoughts were all broken, floating in front of my eyes as small, self-contained but disjointed pieces, which in turn slowed down or raced. There was no distinction between people dead and alive, far and near, events in the past and in the present, and the future was not a possibility any more. I think the concept of a future is too abstract when you have lost touch with reality. Maybe it is self-preservation that you don't think of the future, as basic instinct tells you that from such a superb height you can only fall, and you don't really want to know that.

Rumi still remembers the night of terror when none of us slept and I had been awake round-the-clock for four or five days straight. As day broke, he says I was arguing with the window and *Abbu* was crying in the basement room. I too saw Adil cry but did not question why he was crying, this man who, like *Amma,* never cried. I just rubbed his back and said, "Don't cry. It will be alright soon." It was not the window I talked to, but to those whom I could see beyond. The window separated hard ground from ether and as I stepped off the hard ground on that cold, spring morning, the taxi driver drove us unerringly to the nearest emergency room on the way to Arlanda airport; as it became quite evident that I would not make it to Delhi to talk to Dr N.

Adil had spoken to Dr N, the only person he thought could help; Adil had never seen me like this and *Amma* was not there to counsel him.

He booked tickets for us to go to Delhi, then packed bags for himself, Rumi and me, and called for a taxi to go to Arlanda. By then I had fully entered the third dimension of mania, shouting and arguing with people imaginary and real, and it became quite apparent that I needed medical attention. That is when I heard Adil ask the taxi driver if we could go to the nearest emergency room. At the hospital I heard Adil ask Rumi to go inside and find out; I suppose Adil could not leave me alone in the taxi in that state. Now I think, what could my child, not yet 13, have found out? He came out having found out all that Adil needed to know and they both took me in; I did not resist. I also know that whatever he found out has stayed with him these ten years; recently he was able to go to a hospital in Sweden and handle a psychiatric emergency for himself, despite being alone, despite being afraid. It breaks my heart even as it makes me very proud. Later when I was discharged from hospital, I unpacked the suitcase that Adil had packed for me; inside were three mirror-work cushion covers, a white bed sheet and some random, mismatched clothes including some of Ghazal's clothes, which she had left behind. I laughed through my tears and once again realised the enormous strain Adil was under.

The staff in the front room of the hospital emergency were kind and smiling. Rumi now openly wept in fear, his not yet 13-year-old mind immobilised by what he was seeing, his understanding unable to wrap around it. Adil's silence was a scream that penetrated even my deaf ears. I was acutely aware of this. I was also aware of my state, as of a third person's, and aware that this was a hospital where I was to be treated. It was déjà vu of another state of mind, of another reality altogether, another time, with definite signs of a memory Adil and Rumi were not privy to, and I did not want to share it with them because I knew they could not take it. The doctors met me, ironically, in the ECT room. All signs were in Swedish and I don't recognise the equipment that passes electrical shocks through the brain, but I knew from the starkness of the room and the straps on the bed what this room was meant for. I tried to overcome my fear by being facetious, actually giving the doctors permission to use ECT on me, sharing the exclusive knowledge that it had worked before. They appeared unmoved.

Rumi and Adil saw me being led away, without struggle and without a sound, my big, winter boots striding down the corridor, their thump muted by an emotion that I can only call fear, as I don't know any like it, which imploded in my brain. Adil took Rumi home, wrapped him in a blanket and lay him down on our long lounger. Then he built a big, roaring fire in the fireplace and made him tea. From that day onwards, for a very long time, he was both *Ammi* and *Abbu* to Rumi.

Inside the hospital, the story was different. The staff seemed rude and loud to my heightened senses; they wrenched the coat off my back and pushed me to the ground to 'assist' me with my shoes. I started to shiver although it was really quite warm in the hospital corridors. I asked in English what was to happen next, and one of the attendants asked tauntingly, "Prata du Svenska?" do you speak Swedish, a question asked so often I had even attempted to learn the language. I did not want to offend this guy and I was explicitly afraid of the other one, so I said, "Bara lite," just a little, and kept very quiet lest they found out that I could not speak a word of Swedish, even to save my life. My state of mind seemed a direct affront to them and my lack of Swedish compounded this.

A small room inside had a bed with straps to tie you down with, and this bed was placed diagonally in the middle of the room. I was given a push on my back a few times and dragged to this room. Five men and women held me down on the bed while a sixth and a seventh strapped me down. I tried to tell them that they did not need to tie me and that I would cooperate and take whatever injection they were preparing to give me, when one man turned around and snapped, "Inget Engelska," no English. What had been a slow implosion of fear and anger up to now exploded in my brain and I began to shout in the foulest language, cursing this man and hating this country with a passion. It took all their strength to hold me down. The injection made me pass out, but the boiling wrath bubbled over even when I awoke after several hours. In that state I was locked up in my room and I sat hunched inside the cupboard, crouching like a caged animal, whimpering. Now, thinking back, I wonder if this was an Electroconvulsive treatment they gave me to slow me down. I only remembered the intense headache from the last time and a similar slamming headache was there this time as well. I was still going at breakneck speed. I feel a resentment if it indeed was an ECT, as the need for it was brought about by the attitude of the hospital staff. Anyway, that is something I will never know.

I don't know how much time passed like this, perhaps days. I asked for writing material and wrote a petition trying to convince someone that I should not be here. This petition was handwritten, all in capital letters with no punctuation marks, words running into each other and lines running every which way but horizontal. I was started on Lithium and an antipsychotic, and slowly my thoughts began to untwist themselves.

Then one day Adil came and told me that my petition, written on blue paper, had reached the hospital authorities and that I was to be brought in front of a court of sorts, to present my case. It seemed so ridiculous, but it was deadly serious. An old lady from the hospital staff was on my side and she held both my cold, clammy hands in hers. A very serious looking gentleman explained to me that although my husband and my son had brought me here voluntarily, I was no longer free to go home until the state decided that I am fit to do so. I, of course, had no case since I was still very ill and the medicines were stabilising very slowly, making me groggy and impairing my coordination at the same time. Some time during the hearing I stopped listening and went into a blank stupor. What was there to hear beyond what I had already heard in the opening remarks? That my judgement was impaired. That I was psychotic and had lost touch with reality. That I could do harm to others and to myself. That in bringing me here my husband had committed me to the hospital ward. Committed? Sectioned? Words from long ago reading and cinema flashed through my mind. At least that is what I understood from the old lady's translations whispered in my ear. I gave in to my status as a prisoner and let them lead me back to my cell.

Later I got to know well the young men and women who had mistreated me and cared for me at the same time, and began to understand why a manic episode often evokes a violent response from caretakers, even ones very close to you. It is almost as though they think the symptoms are deliberate and believe, despite themselves, that it is something you can reason out of, pull yourself out of, knowing full well that you can't. It is a reaction, not justifiable, not understandable, but inevitable. It is unreal reality and no one knows where to draw the line.

This episode was different from the first two, certainly very different from the first. At the start when I was still at home, there were hallucinations, in that I could see people at a distance and hear sounds that were not there. I heard Adil talking to his brother outside in the garden, I heard my cousins, scattered all over the US and one in India, laughing and talking in our basement and listening to Bob Dylan, I could see their shadows moving around as on a screen, defying all laws of Physics. Then I went rushing down to hush everyone as Azad was in the room sleeping and must not be woken up. They were all there as well-defined apparitions; only I could not find Azad there; he had left.

In the months preceding I had intoxicated myself on Grateful Dead's Ripple, but there was no music in the last weeks and I was in depression. One evening Adil tried to play some music for me, finding me really disturbed and agitated. The music began to choke me and we had to turn it off. Something unusual was happening; this was not a pure manic episode as I had experienced earlier; instead it was as though the negative components of depression were being carried up, elevated, on the wings of mania. It was mania nonetheless, with its manic energy, its delusions, its surreal hallucinations, unreal, irrational. But it was a mania that had picked up the elements of depression, the sadness, the resentment, the dejection, the perceived rejection by others, the low self-esteem – and shot it up as explosive, deluded, livid anger. This is what Ghazal calls mania in a third dimension of a supposedly two-dimensional bipolar illness, and the psychiatrists call a 'mixed' episode, for want of a better term.

I met many people in the hospital, doctors, patients, nurses, the kitchen staff, the cleaning staff, drug addicts brought in by the police, an older lady who used to sit stark naked at the dining table, a young artist also brought in by the police as he lost it in the town centre. It was very touching to find them all wanting to communicate in their limited English, even the man who had barked out, "No English!" on the first day. They were truly caring and set at rest my need to apologise for the way I was. Yes, many people say you don't have to be sorry for the way you are, for the things you said, but few really mean it. I have learnt along the way not to accept this rather superficial sincerity any more and apologise nonetheless.

I have smoked off and on since I was 12 years old. In times of mental and emotional stress I have always felt the need to smoke and I did this time too, going through packs and packs that an attendant bought and kept in store for me. The psychiatric wing had a walled garden where the staff could smoke. The patients, however, had to contain their smoking to the rather morbid smoking room, which was never touched by daylight and which had violent stains on the wall of unknown origin. The only person who occasionally went out into the garden was my friend Thea, also a patient, but who insisted on calling herself an inmate. She too was brought in by the police, as she had been many times before. She was known for her green thumb and was planting the spring garden. But she too had to come inside to smoke.

On my first drive out for a day trip, Thea gave me the address of a secondhand shop in a town called Sala, where I would find this person who had all the answers. I cannot now construct the questions I wanted answers to, but can still feel the urgency of doing so in my bones. Adil, with Rumi in tow, drove me there. We parked the car and walked up and down the streets of this town, hugging the sparse wintry sunshine along the way, found the shop we were looking for, where I bought a braided ring. There was no person there who I could put the questions to, but I brought back this ring with the firm belief that it would lead me to salvation. I wore this ring for many years.

One day the nurses called me out into the garden. Someone brought my cigarette pack from the store cupboard and they said I could smoke in the garden with them. I was a little nervous I remember, as I was not ready for any kind of normal interaction, but on the whole very pleased. The garden was a pretty picture with the crocuses in full glory and tulips and daffodils just out. Every day I met the nurses outside and slowly began to talk to them about what went on in my mind when I went into a manic episode, how I could hear a whole symphony in the hum of the cooker hood, see a whole lifetime out of the plate glass window of Thuregatan 5, make connections between unrelated events, plausible connections, within a few minutes and a few sentences, feel an instant sense of relatedness to people and things remote – I would tire easily and asked if we could have my friend Thea out as well, as I had already spoken much to her and she could fill in. The answer was a categorical no.

Then one evening, when we were out for our after dinner smoke that stretched into the before bedtime smoke, with many smokes in between, a student nurse gave me a sheaf of lined paper and a pen and asked if I would write down my thoughts and give them to her. She was a student nurse of some sort and wanted to write her paper on the care of bipolar patients. I am a little hazy now, about what exactly she said she would do with my thoughts. At that time I was a little confused too as to what was required of me. That made me nervous and my hands began to tremble violently as I started to smoke one cigarette after another. By then there were several doctors out as well. Very gently the seniormost nurse amongst them, normally a quite forbidding lady of my age, took matters into her hands. She explained that in their experience I was one of very few patients who had such a clear recollection of manic episodes, even from the past, and one who could relate thoughts, emotions and feelings with such focus and clarity, in a way that it was even understood by those members of staff who had limited English.

For the first time in the 29-year-life of my illness I felt that perhaps, my understanding of myself and this affliction, my acute memory, were not in vain, not such a curse after all. In my situation it is not really a positive thing to remember everything and I had often wished I could forget. I did write some notes on those sheets of paper, but my mind was weak and those notes could not have been very coherent. They let me go home for the night a couple of times. As Adil was travelling on work, our friend Kerri took me home and cooked dinner for Rumi and me. She was a little nervous about being able to handle my irrational thoughts and actions. The nurse on duty said, "Just disagree with all irrational thoughts and restrain all irrational actions." Fortunately she only had to disagree. And finally, the state saw fit that I go home. The senior nurse came out to the taxi and said to me, "Write a book and send us a copy."

Little did she know that I would be back in a few months and would bring with me masses of paper with stuff written all over it that no one could understand, not even I.

The summer of 2007 was spent with the children at Woodsong in Bangalore. I was still very shaky and on heavy medication and all three were invariably kind. Before leaving Sweden I had gone back parttime to my teaching job, but it felt as though it was not going to work. I was terribly slowed down and being the way I was, it was virtually impossible to enthuse the small group of middle schoolers in my care. At Woodsong there was time, quiet and space to dwell on the future and slowly I felt my strength and courage return. From this far away it seemed I could return to Sweden, pick up the threads of my life and go back to teaching.

Back in Sweden Dr ES was very pleased with my progress and talked about recovery. As is the practice in Sweden, I had a long wait before I could get an appointment to see her and was communicating with her through her nurse practitioner. During a long, first interview she felt I was reasonable and in touch with the real issues of my state. She also felt I was not at all psychotic and, therefore, it would be quite safe to take me off Abilify, an atypical antipsychotic drug. I was significantly encouraged, as I related events of the 23 years of coping without psychiatric help or drugs. She was visibly impressed, but quite firmly refused to take me off Lithium immediately. Perhaps later. As in the US, she strongly recommended that I continue on a maintenance dose of Lithium for life. This disturbed me somewhat, but I was still fresh from the helpless flailing of the recent episode and did not argue. Active memory of those 23 years was fast receding in the wake of the months just gone by and my calm demeanour that appeared to be a steady, euthymic emotional state, was actually a descent into depression.

After I met the psychiatrist, I wrote in a letter to Ghazal and Azad:

~

Hi Ghazal and Azad, my babies,

I can see that you have gone to sleep, at least I hope you have gone to sleep. I have been planning to write this letter since Monday, but I find that I still keep mulling on things rather than just doing them. But it's getting better I think.

Sunday pretty much went in cleaning the house after the German kids left. There were occasions when Rumi was quite annoyed with them, but on the whole he was quite sad that the week ended. It was actually like a weeklong party and so, of course, this week the 8c attendance is quite low. Rumi has dragged himself to school the last three days, but looked quite ill today and has stayed in bed. I am beginning to get a little concerned about this tiredness.

(That was a few days ago, and I have been trying to write more since then.)

My tiredness persists and I don't understand it. It is incapacitating and debilitating. The intensive Chemistry in Swedish that I help Rumi with makes my head hurt. The Maths lessons in school that are usually my pride and joy, are dry and unimaginative; though adequate, even if barely so. All creativity appears to be snuffed out and everything is exacting, tedious and joyless. It does leave me wondering what it will take to make things alright.

Twice this week I had to go to the hospital, but not because anything is wrong. I just don't like going to the hospital. The first time was to do a blood test for lithium levels. The second visit on Wednesday was to see my doctor. Her name is Dr ES and she is quite a remarkable lady, about 70 years old, with a matter of fact, no-nonsense approach and a kindly manner that I truly appreciate. I had many questions for her, although I knew all along that she would not have many answers for me; whatever abnormal psychology I have studied (and can remember) tells me that there are no real answers to many of these questions, but I asked my questions anyway. She was very patient and talked to me for a long time. She confirmed that at this stage it is very hard to tell whether the feeling of being trapped in my mind, the lack of creativity, the feelings of tiredness and despondency, the deadened senses, are symptoms of the continuing illness or they are there because of the effect and side effects of the medicine and actually indicate growing wellness under the influence of the drug. I don't know how to process this, or what I would want it to be if I were given a choice; sometimes I would rather it were a part of the illness, as then there is hope of getting better. To accept that this is what being well is going to be like, while one grows increasingly dependent on Lithium, is to reconcile to a bland and faceless existence. A frightening thought.

I also talked to her about giving up Lithium sometime soon. The default prescription of Lithium after a major episode like this is for life, to rule out a recurrence. In the late '70s in India, this illness was not very well documented and Lithium was not in use, and everything just got horribly messed up; a recurrence was inevitable. Twenty-three years ago the US doctors gave me a lifetime prescription and painted a very bleak picture of what would happen if I went off Lithium. I fought against it, and worked very hard to go off all drugs and stay off them. I did not read Kay Jamison until much later and I don't know if this would have changed my stance. Here too, the Swedish doctors have suggested a lifetime maintenance dose of Lithium. This doctor thankfully has some faith in the human mind and is willing to let me consider reducing lithium levels very, very slowly after autumn; actually more towards the end of the year, or in early 2008. It will take time; months, maybe more, and she explained the risks to me. I already know the risks and have never really been afraid. Yet now I am and that concerns me.

Meri jaan, the decisions are mine to take and I must find the courage to take them. I do realise that I am troubled by it right now, but this would be no harder than the many choices I have had to make before, some against all odds; and then I worked with them successfully. At least I hope so. Had another bit of a setback, though. Just heard from a friend I had made in the hospital, Andreas. He tried to go off Lithium and had a massive recurrence. That has scared him for sure, but it has shaken me terribly.

In the meantime, I continue trying to read and to listen to music. Oh, it is just not happening. Am also trying to increase my workload to 75 per cent. I reckon if I do more work it will keep my mind off itself. Except that I am apparently doing the maximum I am capable of.

I love you both very much,

Ammi

~

A descent into autumn

Take me on a trip upon your magic swirling ship
My senses have been stripped
My hands can't feel to grip
My toes too numb to step
Wait only for my boot heels to be wandering
I'm ready to go anywhere, I'm ready for to fade
Into my own parade
Cast your dancing spell my way,
I promise to go under it

Bob Dylan

Summer ran out quite quickly and the light in the sky dimmed, whilst a quietness began to descend. I found comfort in the rust of the leaves and the grey skies, which seemed more in sync with my low state. The brightness of the summer, both in India and in Sweden, had become very tiring with its joyous bonhomie that appeared superficial, almost a falsity that I could not keep up with, did not want to deal with. I was buried deep under emotional trauma, my steps were heavy and speech sluggish, and the quick witted and glib people around me were making me dizzy. I am told this is what I do to others when I am hurtling towards a manic episode, but at this time I was barely dragging myself towards normalcy.

As the days shortened and darkened I stayed shut in the house most of the time, not doing much, not talking at all. I used to walk to school once a day, everyday, not even on 75% work yet, already dreading the upcoming cold and darkness. The school, the children, Adil, Kerri were

all very kind, but my restlessness and uneasiness continued unabated.
In the silence of my soul. I wrote poetry.

~

<u>blue</u>

in front of the cupboard in unquiet despair
aware of each nerve in the body,
each perception in the mind
and its resonance in the heart.

the eyes searched for the colour blue,
the hands reached for a blue sweater.

the electric blue of an alpine sky above pristine clouds
like large mounds of snow, dense, white and unyielding
even to the powerful thrust of the aeroplane engine
or the sharp eye of a camera lens.

the deep, cobalt blue of the turkish mediterranean,
where it meets the crystal green of more shallow waters
and is reflected in the kind, blue eyes
of the refugee lady from kosovo,
as she knitted warm socks for cold feet,
on that faraway summer's night that was freezing.

the blue on tiles that make the rise of a stairway
to a heaven sought,

but is numbed with pain and exhaustion

into a nameless fear

that took the place of an overwhelming sadness that had become
unbearable.

the same blue on a ceramic mug

that holds a small bunch of orange nasturtiums,

picked on a day filled with sunshine,

but one that only serves as a reminder of a child,

not allowed to draw its first breath, lost, yet perhaps not forever.

to drive away the blues, what a strange thought, almost thoughtless.

still, the blue colour faded from an aerogramme,

the air letter folder of a long time ago,

with its carefully calligraphed words in royal blue ink

that scattered in front of the eyes,

even as they could not be formed.

it may yet become another 'blue letter from home' as life,

and the colour blue, are so very precious.

~

<u>For you precious, the second day of a new week</u>

Snow pants from the hallway cupboard; woollen socks from a Kosovar
lady, a gift on the streets of Istanbul on a freezing summer's night many
years ago; snow tyres on the bicycle.

I read a poem about a mother, and blossoms and snow, and silence,

I read a letter from a grandmother

And a single line from miles away, filled with the sweetness of rich, dark chocolate infused with an orange freshness.

And saw the amber light of a quiet champion who'd rather walk his path alone, but leave the sound of his footsteps in every silent moment.

I read my own handwriting too, of words that wouldn't form.

The dry twig extends its arm from a mound of snow; dried in the shortening days of autumn,

and ravaged by the lengthening nights of a winter that bluntly refused to come in all its sparkling glory,

Of crystalline snowflakes that blinded and numbed at first, but now crunch under warm boots and break the deafening silence.

The twig still snaps, but its despairing crack of yesterday is gently and warmly softened by the cold hand of snow.

And it is allowed to reach for the sky

That quietly stepped out of a holy night and broke into daylight this morning, with its soft hues of orange and pink; and this gracefully gave way to a soothing grey that would not

Allow its nature to be determined by its name or its colour.

~

And so it went on, into pages and pages. I had a MacBook that was just a few months old and many hours were spent learning how to use it, how to write on it, how to access and use the internet. It began with writing my 'stuff' on it and reading on the internet about bipolar disorder and the various drugs used to treat it. There is really only so much to read about that and I must have read every article or blog a layman can comprehend. Then late into the night I would cruise on the internet, marvelling at what all people had to say, not minding who read it. I read some pieces that were actually quite brilliant, others pompous or downright idiotic. By then I could no longer read anything with substance or length and found relief in these quick reads. Without knowing, my mind got sucked into the internet and I began to create an alternative reality there, began to find meaning where none existed, began to interpret my life in the arbitrary words I read. Unknown to me, or anyone else for that matter, my mind began to fly once again, from the depths of depression past any semblance of momentary normalcy straight into delusions induced by the internet; delusions of affecting the lives of people whose posts I read; delusions of my influence on the world at large as represented on the internet. It is a small mercy that I did not know how to write a post. But it all came out in emails I wrote to everybody I knew. It still took a long time for it to be found out that I was re-entering the manic space.

Then there was the church craze; I wanted to buy an old church painted the lovely Swedish red with a white trim and build my home in it. We went all about the countryside looking for a church that fit our needs and budget. I am astonished at the way Adil and the children went along with me, how they made it their dream, their reality. There was, of course, an enormous sense of relief when this did not come about. It has left me, however, with this longing every time I see a red and white church in Sweden.

I don't have such a clear recollection of this episode, except that there was far less anger, fewer feelings of grandeur, more paranoia, only some passing hallucinations in the beginning and a ready acceptance of the return to hospital. Unfortunately the hospital decided to put me in a different ward with a different regimen and this totally threw me off. Anger welled up at small things. For example, this ward allowed patients to bring their own toothbrushes but the toothpaste was rationed out twice a day! I grew obstinate and refused the medicines unless they gave me the chemical break up and side effects of each drug. They did allow me to bring in my laptop, but without internet access. Late into the night I listened to music on my laptop and refused to sleep.

I believe it was reported that I was a very difficult patient and I was sent back to the familiar environs of the earlier ward, meant for difficult patients. The attitude of the staff was not so kind again and I lashed out with physical violence at being refused food in the middle of the night. The security was called in and I was locked up, not even allowed to go to the bathroom. I wet my sheet and tore it into thin strips. Then I lay on the bare ground under the window and passed out shivering violently, without a pillow under my head or a blanket to keep me warm. I am told that I slept for a day and a half. I woke up with a heavy head to find that my bed had been moved to where the afternoon sun came in; there were fresh blanket and sheets on the bed and my clothes had been changed. I stole one of the sheets as a memento, a birthday present.

Without the usual anticipation of a birthday, without anyone to wish me, without even the most modest of celebrations I had turned fifty.

Adil came to wish me and brought me a Montblanc ballpoint. All I could do was weep, saying, this is not how it is supposed to be. The pen sat in its box, an odd and somewhat contradictory reminder of the terrible time and of Adil's thoughtfulness, and now I cannot seem to find it. I could not bring myself to use it, but every time I saw it, I felt that split second gratitude that there were remnants of normal emotion at that time and I had not lost all touch with reality.

This was an easier term in the hospital, I forget for how long. As they allowed my laptop, I wrote a little. A young student was brought in, in very bad shape. He was an artist and a poet and I was allowed to mentor him. We became good friends. Before the first snow I was discharged from the hospital. Azad and Ghazal made a quick visit when I came home, but I was still very ill. Then they came to Sweden for Christmas and to usher in the new year, and found a significantly depleted *Ammi*, a tired *Abbu* and a younger brother grown beyond his years. Other than the times I could contain myself no longer and broke down crying, we shared our troubles and emotions in utter silence. The year 2008 came and then went, without as much as a murmur.

Slow and weary

Though I know that evening's empire has returned into sand
Vanished from my hand
Left me blindly here to stand but still not sleeping
My weariness amazes me, I'm branded on my feet
I have no one to meet
And the ancient empty street's too dead for dreaming

Bob Dylan

In the summer of 2009, with the storm of my emotions lulled by Lithium and an antipsychotic, and when the almost round-the-clock daylight was unable to lift my spirits, we sold Thuregatan 5, put all our belongings into a container, and moved to Switzerland. Many have said to me that I must not want to ever return to Sweden again. That is simply not true. The time spent in Sweden was very precious; it brought out emotions that would not have come out anywhere in the world, leaving behind a sweet, *lagom* ache, an ache which is neither too much nor too little. Rumi agrees with me. We moved to a house in Maur outside Zurich, in the midst of horse farms set in pristine countryside. It was like living in a picture postcard; but I was oblivious to that. I was oblivious to sights and sounds, to colour and music, to love and affection, even to my children. Rumi felt it the most as he was with us all through and I wonder what he felt, wonder what he thought of the person I had become. He learnt to wash his own clothes, cook his food, shop for clothes and build himself a value system of right and wrong unassisted by me, unshared with me. The cataclysmic trauma of the last years sat inside him like a knot around his heart, a smouldering ball of fire inside, waiting to erupt and break his heart.

The apparent reason to move was Adil's job, but another reason, which was less apparent and not even discussed, was that this move may serve to provide me with a change of scene that could perhaps bring me out of my stupor. It was a painless stupor as it asked for nothing, not even to come out of itself. There was just a dull, not so unpleasant ache that told me I was still alive. On the outside it looked somewhat like the depression after my first episode, but on the inside it was nothing like that. There was a kernel of emotional energy still left in me, a minuscule amount that allowed me to go about a bare minimum of living.

Then there was Rumi and I could not just abandon him, even in the state I was. Every morning I got up with the alarm and made breakfast and lunch for him, every afternoon I stood by the kitchen window and waited for his bus. In the kitchen was a digital clock that gave me numbers to swirl in my head and find the good in the thoughts in my head at that moment or the events that happened at a specific time. A little difficult to explain. If I got up at night at 01:04 to drink a glass of water, that was good, as Rumi was born in 0104 Regent Garden. Also, I was told long back that in Chinese numerology 0104 stood for 'every day you die.' It was immaterial if it was 01:07 instead; 19:57 and 19:58 were good times to have dinner, 16:16 a good time for Rumi's bus to come, and recently I came upon 00:00 when awake past midnight and that was very good; it nullified everything! Reasons for according some numbers and times with a special significance are too numerous and too vague to describe. The reasons don't matter; the fact that I filled the gaping void in my mind with such an unintelligent and spurious activity does. Thankfully there were no bad numbers. 13, 666, 9/11 were all numbers of significance, and so, good. 14, 777, 10/11 were inconsequential. Now had it been 007, James Bond, that would have been so good! And I travelled for my lunches with John on the 747 bus, a jet aeroplane. My last, highly negative, hypomanic episode, much later in time, brought into play the date 11/11/11. I wrote intense and bizarre emails; then, since I was unable to schedule an appointment at 11:11 with the psychiatrist I was seeing at the time, I arrived at her door at exactly this time and had a lengthy, 'reasonable' discussion/argument with her. By evening I was incensed with unreal and irrational thoughts and Adil had a difficult time convincing her that I was really very ill, no matter what I had said to her and how I seemed that morning. Fortunately I had warned her of this possibility, told her that if I wanted to hide my state from her I could, and therefore, what Adil said was to take precedence over what I said, at all times. Adil is the barometer for the state of my mind and is not to be fooled by how I choose to be seen by others. I still furtively look at numbers on the oven clock and they bring a covert smile to my lips. It is a harmless *shaghal, a* pastime, and rarely, if ever, becomes psychotic; it is like a positive version of Tehmina's mercury retrograde.

While Rumi was in school I sat on a chair or lay in bed, completely devoid of feelings, and picked my nose. There were no dark thoughts or racing thoughts; in fact thoughts were conspicuous by their absence. There was no movement of time and the long day slowly passed in a small instance. When Rumi came home I made him a snack and sometimes he would wordlessly take it to his basement room. He was hurting and the occasional, pretended conversations were more hurtful; I knew why, but there was nothing I could do about it, as I did not have the capacity, either for meaningful talk or to feel hurt. Again I wonder, what did he make of all this? Every evening, at the same time, I cooked a vegetable, some *daal* and *rotis.* I have cooked *rotis* ever since and found that the process calms me down. At that time all this was done mechanically, unemotionally, without any enthusiasm, leave alone passion. There was not the slightest emotional flutter to be calmed. I slept the whole night, every night, and yet felt incredibly tired. I was not sad, I did not cry, had no thoughts of suicide or of the future. On weekends I was dragged around by Adil and Rumi. The house had to be cleaned and I helped Adil vacuum and wash the bathrooms. Then we went out to a large grocery store and got a week's worth of provisions. I went passively and wheeled the cart. That winter Adil removed the snow from the drive on his own, and cut the grass before and after, in autumn and spring, also on his own. Our close friends, Lily and John, who lived in another village, came sometimes. John would meet me for lunch during the week, a practice that has continued to this day and is one of my greatest joys; he would painstakingly explain the bus and tram routes to me in precise detail, so I wouldn't get lost. Dr ES, back in Sweden, had explained to me that if I can look forward to something, then I am not so acutely depressed. I certainly looked forward to these lunches and remember coming out of myself a little bit to chat during the meal. Another friend came to take me for a walk in the surrounding countryside. I went along without resistance. I have asked people later what they remember me as, during this time; without exception they have said, "You just sat and did not say anything."

It was a benign sort of depression that has left no mark on my memory. I don't remember the address of the house in Maur where we lived, or even its arrangement of rooms, which keeps getting mixed up with the layout of our beautiful home in Sweden. I rarely moved out of the house and cannot recollect the routes of trams and buses that I must have taken occasionally. It was a still year with not a ripple. Many years later we have moved back to Zurich and I am surprised at how little I know of the city, so little that there have been only occasional and fleeting feelings of déjà vu; the rest is pleasurable discovery made with new strengths of my mind.

Parvarish

You who are on the road
Must have a code that you can live by
And so become yourself
Because the past is just a goodbye.

Teach your children well,
Their father's hell did slowly go by,
And feed them on your dreams
The one they pick's the one you'll know by.
Don't you ever ask them why, if they told you, you will cry,
So just look at them and sigh
And know they love you.

And you, of tender years,
Can't know the fears that your elders grew by,
And so please help them with your youth,
They seek the truth before they can die.

Crosby, Stills, Nash and Young

Parvarish is to bring up, nurture. During the 23-year-window of 'sanity' that I had been granted and also in the following troubled years, Adil and I brought up three gorgeous children. Or perhaps I should say that Adil brought me up single-handedly after *Amma* died, making good his promise that he will care for me as no one else. This he did with a firm kindness and infinite patience, so he and I could bring up our children.

I know every mother thinks her children are the most wonderful beings, and I am no different; but my children are. They have taken a hold of my distorted reality and have made it their own, each according to his or her own very unique personality. Much to our psychiatrist's chagrin and dismay, they almost proudly tell people how crazy I am and most fondly transfer this epithet to their father as well, one of the sanest persons on earth. Or maybe there is an element of induced aberration in Adil that allows him to deal with so much deviation from the norm. Yet some privileges are mine alone, attributed to the fact that I am different. Rumi has said to his friends more than once, "If you think I am crazy, wait till you meet my mother."

One evening we were at the Golf Club. No one plays golf in our family, yet we retained membership because of their crispy *gobhi* manchurian with ginger, garlic and chilli wrapped close around it and their caramel pudding with the mint leaf crowning it, which are out of this world. Otherwise the club is as stuffy as the best of them. That evening we took some guests for dinner. Rumi was six years old and we were very cognisant of the club rule that children under 12 must leave by 9 pm or 10 pm, I forget which. I ordered his food first, but of course as luck would have it, it came last, and he was still wrapping his noodles perfunctorily on his fork when everyone finished eating and it was past the time he should have left. To save time I thought I'd get the bill. The waiter brought a fancy box that he flipped open in front of me. Inside, instead of the bill, were rolled up company rules of the club. I was overwrought and intensely 'explained' to the concierge as we left, why we could not leave on time. Ghazal said to our nonplussed guests, "Don't worry. *Ammi* is *Don Amma*; many a company has changed policies after she has been at them." Azad said, not too harshly, that I need not have spoken to them like that and Rumi would have said, "That's rude," if he was old enough to decipher the biting sarcasm in my tone and words. Adil said nothing, but I know he was not particularly proud of me at such moments, yet willing to accept me the way I was. Sometimes I would even see a begrudging admiration flit across his face.

With Ghazal I go often to the opening night at this art gallery behind our house, because they serve free alcohol! Once Adil asked if she went for the art or the alcohol and we had to tell him she sometimes misses the art altogether. Rumi said with a quizzical expression on his face, "Funny girl! First she goes to the art gallery for free booze, and then she takes her mother along." With Ghazal I am just a habit, started when she was very young. Her *Amma Nani* and I used to laugh at her and say, *"Ammi tu hi bata de," Ammi,* you tell. *Amma* used to sometimes call her *'ullu ki dum fakhta,'* which literally translates to owl's tail dove. I have no idea what that really means, but it seems to suggest an absurdity of absurdities. Ghazal was unabashed when I taught her class Physics in high school; she just sat in the back of the room and often raised her hand, saying, "But *Ammi...*" No one sniggered; and even if someone had, it would not have mattered to her. She was strangely insulated from outside ridicule.

When she was two and Azad had just started nursery school, we sent Ghazal to a neighbouring day care for a couple of hours each day, so she would be with others outside the family. She went, unwillingly at first, but soon with growing enthusiasm. She was not yet talking or doing anything for herself. At the daycare they taught her to shower, change, wear her shoes, eat on her own; this in addition to an extensive reading and writing curriculum in Malay and English. Leave alone reading and writing, which was a bit ridiculous anyway, Ghazal did not carry any of her learning home. One day when I went to fetch her, grave caretakers met me at the gate. Ghazal had bitten a Chinese boy on the cheek. Everyone had thought she was going to kiss him, but she bit him, bit him hard. I walked her home and was angry with her. Then I tried to explain to her that it was wrong, asked her if she was angry about something, asked if the boy had upset her; but she could not tell me anything, as she could not talk. She was not ashamed, or sad, or upset, and simply loped around the house like she always did. The next day I took her back to the day care and she bit him again, this time harder still. It became a serious issue. When I brought her back I just held her close to me and crooned to her, sang Joseph's face (Under African Skies by Paul Simon) to her, played Daldi (Vivaldi) to her, sang her my lullaby: *'nanhi kali soney chali, hava dheerey aana, neend bharey rang liye, jhoola jhula jaana,'* tiny flower bud is off to sleep, breeze come gently; bring colours filled with slumber, to rock the baby asleep; then showered her, dressed her, tied her shoelaces and very tentatively we walked back to the daycare the next day. And it was all well again, just like that. I have often wondered what was going on inside this child's head, this mildest of mild children.

She was a balmy creature, not yet seven when Rumi was born, who viewed the world through warm, limpid eyes, a world she did not quite fit into. She had her own imaginary world, filled with people who were real to her, friends whom she loved and conversations that held all the meaning for her. One warm, sunny morning three of her friends took off from a hotel window in Oklahoma. She ran to the window and looking at the sky, called out most unselfconsciously, "Arado, Barado, Garado, are you all right? Do you have money?" Satisfied with whatever reply she got, she went back to the table and finished her breakfast of cereal and milk.

Primary school was a happy place for Ghazal. She was at a school where a third of its population was coping with mild to severe mental, physical or emotional challenges, so there were not many odd ones out. Ghazal simply did what she could or wanted to, and did not do what she could not or did not want to. That was just fine with us. She was a pro at reading. I had read aloud to her constantly when she had not started reading, and by the time Rumi was born she was reading Asimov. She didn't like anybody to teach her anything. If, while reading to her, I skimmed my finger over a word, trying to draw her attention to it, she would still my hand and say, "Just read to me, don't point at the words." When reading aloud to Rumi later, I had learnt to only read.

We felt she should do more physical activity, so I enrolled her in several after school activities. With two left feet and arms that got in the way she performed gymnastics with the dedication of an olympic gymnast, leisurely strolled behind kids running after a football, used her immense mental strengths to master several levels of karate, played basketball and cricket without regard to how she was doing and came last in every single race. Competition was not a word in her lexicon and she shed no tears over what she could not do. No one said anything to us and we said nothing to her.

Until one day the Art teacher said to us, "If you want to see Ghazal in sheer agony, visit our Art class." Ghazal could not stand the paint, the glue, the little bits of paper that stuck to her fingers. (Much later, when applying for university admissions, she rejected admission to Reed because they sent her confetti in their admissions package. She said she didn't want to go where they celebrated with little bits of coloured paper!) She spent her entire time fretting in the Art class and then fled the moment she could. This Art teacher was a kind and wise woman and she made Ghazal the project designer and director, so that she would continue to be involved, but did not have to touch the messy stuff. Later, in middle school, her then Art teacher was complaining to us that we never came to the Art Village to see Ghazal's work. Ghazal had done no work at the Art Village and Adil said, with a deadpan face, "We don't come because art has a silent F." The poor man sheepishly laughed, we hope because he didn't understand, and Ghazal looked like she wanted the ground to swallow her.

Ghazal hated birthdays when she was growing up. Many birthdays were in Aligarh, as she was born in December and that was the time for our annual visit. That meant birthday parties with a motley crew of children and party games. As the number of people grew she would withdraw into a corner or sit back to back with me, with a book, and gently rock herself. Many commented that she was a strange girl, '*ajeeb ladki hai,*' who didn't want to join in the fun. She gave the impression she did not hear what was said and just waited for everyone to leave. She opened her presents when asked to do so and with an adult's falsity exclaimed,

"Oh, look at this!" and "Oh my!" then left the gifts in a debris of shredded wrapping paper, never to touch them again.

There were other things too: For years she walked like a duck, with her feet spread out in a wide V. All the way back from Auckland she did the 'haka,' the traditional Maori war cry, at immigration, at the customs, to the air hostesses, even for the taxi driver back in Singapore. She would constantly act out Peter Pan, her favourite character, at the most inopportune times. She would often talk about death: that she was never going to die, as she was never going to grow up, but her *Amma Nani* would. Once she asked *Amma* how old she was, and got obsessed with the fear that she would die soon. She doesn't wear socks of the same colour. She doesn't go to a hairdresser but cuts her own hair with blunt scissors in front of the bathroom mirror. (This, I suspect, comes from Adil, who also cuts his own hair; but he owns every conceivable hair cutting tool!)

This was Ghazal's reality and we never corrected her. Adil and I, however, had to school ourselves in our perception of this reality. For us she remained, first and foremost, caring, someone who would go many extra miles for those she cared about. And she is wonderfully intelligent, in an almost playful way.

When Ghazal reached the second grade, the Head Teacher of the Centre for Special Education approached me in the school corridor and asked if he could speak to me. I said, "Of course," thinking it had to do with one of the special needs students who had been integrated into mainstream. It turned out he wanted to speak to me about Ghazal. He said he would like to have Ghazal tested, as sometimes it was really impossible to have her even attempt certain tasks. One such task was writing and she was firm in her inability and refusal to write, emphatic that she didn't need to and politely ticked off her teacher for insisting that she should try. The other was social, as Ghazal liked to be by herself; not in a hostile manner, but just as a preference. The Art we already knew about. All this suggested that she had some kind of a learning/psychological difficulty.

I went home and told Adil. He was alarmed by this idea and flew off the handle, saying no one was going to test his daughter. She was made differently, yes, but this was not harming her nor harming anyone else. There ended the matter as far as he was concerned. I was afraid too, whether she was tested or not, knowing I would have to do something about it. I looked at my child; polite, contained, correct, mature; who just couldn't do certain things. That acknowledgement spearheaded the courage and determination to fight this. Every waking hour when she was home, I worked with her, breaking up the unpleasant tasks into bite-size bits and patiently waiting for her consent to try. I never insisted that she do anything against her will; with slight reservation perhaps, but with her agreement nonetheless.

And I made deals. Rumi once commented that the worst punishment I could mete out was to take away their books. I would never do that, but my agreement with Ghazal was that before she took her next book to read, she had to write a review of the last, according to a format I gave her. How quickly those reviews got written then, in a four line notebook! Her handwriting looked like someone had dipped an ant in ink and let it loose on writing paper; it still does, but with time it has become minimally legible.

I was reading Somebody Somewhere by Donna Williams, an account of her autism and the journey to overcome her affliction. Later I read Nobody Nowhere as well, a prequel to Somebody Somewhere. I did not read these books because I thought Ghazal was autistic, although I could find much in the books that applied to her. Rather, I took the courage to enter the mind of a person with boxed-in feelings and emotions, trapped in a world of random thought patterns and hallucinatory images, without a sense of self with which to relate to others, because I found similar and equally random, though distinct thoughts during my manic attacks, trapped and suffocated emotions during depression, and a depleted self at all times. Later I met a child who was supposed to have Asperger's syndrome, another who had ADHD and then Rumi who was diagnosed bipolar, a friend's son who got addicted to Xanax, a nephew who was habituated to weed, several, young and old, dependent on alcohol, two autistic brothers, and the list goes on, with, as Ghazal points out, many states in between and overlapping. Each of these have their own behaviour patterns, their descriptors, which help identify them, but underlying all of these is anxiety, fear, lack of motivation, lowered self-esteem, depression – no medical doctor can really treat these. *Amma* told a story from her Child Development class. A poor woman gave full term birth to a small, underweight, weak child at a big hospital. The doctors kept the child in an incubator and then in a sterile ward. The mother could only look in through a peephole once a day. Several days passed and there was no improvement, so the hospital asked the woman to come and take her child. The woman clasped her baby to her bosom, which was none to clean, and took him home. The child flourished. We too clasped Ghazal to our bosom. However, Ghazal was not suffering. If my child was suffering, as Rumi later was, I would go right back to the doctor; I would go to a professional, medical doctor first, to rule out an illness and only then work my way down to other forms of therapy.

By then we had moved to Nepal Park, to a classic Singaporean black and white house I had dreamt of living in for almost ten years. While I made *rotis* I watched Ghazal conjure up all kinds of mathematical patterns in the intricate black and white pattern of kitchen tiles. Oblivious to who was watching, she would skip and roll, not touch a black triangle here or a white square there, and make squiggly notes on kitchen paper. Then she would do something really funny, She would hold tight to the sides of the door frame with her hands and feet and climb up the doorway like a four-legged spider; then survey the kitchen floor from there to gain perspective on her work. Sometimes she climbed up other doorways, just for fun, and could carry on an entire conversation hanging from there.

Times tables were a problem and it took a long time to wean her off successive addition. "Why can't I do it this way if I do it quickly enough?" Every evening when I took Rumi in his pram for a stroll, we set up a rhythm for Ghazal on her roller blades, so she could sing out her multiplication tables. The more difficult ones were pasted all over her bathroom walls for the extra long potty time. The rhythmic motion of the roller blades and the swing and sway of her body stayed her mind. She says she never looked at the cards in the bathroom, so I suppose looking past the cards brought them into focus, like bright spots, and without her realising it, they entered her memory.

The adult Ghazal has a rare beauty and serenity about her, like her Mariam *Khala* and *Amma Nani*. She thinks like a scientist and feels like a poet. Sometimes it feels as though she has a special affective intelligence which allows her to feel intensely, without being needlessly sentimental. Whatever a quarter of a century has done that we did not allow the school to do, Ghazal is an erudite research scholar working on some abstract concept in Biophysics that I don't understand, and wonder of wonders, still uses a fountain pen to hand write; all three of our children do. To top this, she is a passionate cook; all three of our children are. She is no longer afraid of messy, sticky substances and dives into wet ingredients, hands first, when she cooks; and hardly ever uses a fork or a spoon. She still lopes about the house, lives in a world of books that she lines up at the edge of her bed and lives in some tense other than the present, but when you need her to be there, she always is.

What can I say of the boys? They drink endless cups of tea with me, as I did with my *Amma,* and Azad did with his *Mammijan,* Adil's mother, and *Nanphu,* my father's sister. In this scalding, amber brew, we find alleviation. They have their father's widow's peaks, his broad forehead, which does not get furrowed, except under extreme provocation. They also have their father's unquestioning belief that having a mental illness does not make you less than who you are. I have to remind Rumi of this sometimes, when he feels less than others. Every single one of his achievements is all the more valuable because of the courage and determination it took to accomplish it.

Azad, our oldest, turns 33 this autumn and his personality has the coolness of an autumn breeze rustling the orange and brown leaves on the ground, infusing them with a life and warmth, entreating them not to wither away. I have known people of all ages and backgrounds to come and bare their troubled souls to him; he only listens, but somehow it brings them a measure of comfort. I copy him on much of my writing; again he never says anything, but it is comforting to know that he reads what I write. He appears a *Sajjada Nashin,* the descendant of a *Sufi* or *Pir,* as his forebears were.

Azad was a grown adult from the moment he was born, self-assured and mature. The little four year old would follow me around, weaving wonderful stories as I did my house chores. In his stories he was always the hero, the leader, battling the problems of the world. *"Lekin Ammi, aur koi tariqa bhi to nahin hai pani band karne ka,"* but *Ammi,* there is no other way to turn the water off, went his story, in which he was called upon to arrest the flooding of his preschool classroom. In later years he wrote these stories down and kept them in the cabin trunk at Woodsong, alongside his term papers and other school work. I sometimes read these stories and papers, but always put them back in the trunk.

As an undergraduate Azad studied Design and Architecture and although he never interfered, he was always there to turn to when designing and building Woodsong. He would give all his attention to the many, knotty problems my engineer and I could not solve. We knew we would come away with sound advice that would not detract from the integrity of the design I had in mind. It was *Ammi's* design, so he did not needlessly add his own elements to it. Some found their way in, nonetheless, reflective of his ancestral home in Lucknow, the *daalan dar daalan,* verandah within verandah, to accord a greater degree of privacy without always having to shut the door. I have an aversion to locked doors, but utmost respect for an individual's privacy and did not know how to incorporate this sentiment into the design. He also designed the skylights and if you lie under them the sky comes in, with the light of the moon or the setting sun. When Saif, our friends' son, visited, he said, "This is surreal."

Even as Woodsong entered its second phase of construction and he began to spend time writing, Azad decided to digress from design and architecture and turn to the study of Abnormal Psychology. His finely tuned mind and a balanced, harmonious temperament were ideal ground for the study of mental and emotional abnormalities. He knew I never had the courage to take on a full course of study in this subject and some part of him wanted to make up for what I could not do, so I could live vicariously through the academic strengths he gained. I suspect it was also so he could know more about the features of the mind that make his younger brother, Rumi and me the way we are.

There is a picture of him that hangs in his grandparents' home, in a white *kurta pyjama,* with a cigarette in one hand and a book on his lap. That is how I know him best, at home anywhere in the world and bringing the world in to where he is. Every room in our house is lined with books, but in his room the books are holding up the walls and ceiling. As in Rumi's room. In Ghazal's room books line the bed and the floor as well!

Rumi takes me along to all the new films that come out. I barely understand these films, but eat popcorn and drink the poisonous cold drink in a PET bottle with great relish. Once we went into gold class cinema and he allowed me to snore in the plush, red velvet seat; the seats recline and they give you blankets, and as Rumi said, I would not have understood very much of the film anyway. A while back we saw Narnia II. Having seen Narnia I, I was just getting into the story and really enjoying myself when Rumi nudged me, "This is really awful, let's leave." I have my own style of film I like to watch, but I would trade that any day to sit by Rumi and watch him laugh and grow serious as he watches his film.

Their friends accept me too, with a warmth that is devoid of any hint of pretence, a warmth that I cannot fully describe. Ghazal and Azad live in an apartment in the north of the city, with several housemates. They sometimes call Rumi and me over, to cook for us the foods they themselves want to eat, and make us tea pungent with ginger and black pepper, respecting the fact that I don't like the cardamom of the typical *masala chai*. One is a writer and he allows me to sometimes read what he writes and grants me the privilege to comment. Their German housemate bakes us the most amazing cakes that are low in sugar and fat. Ghazal tells me that their friends really like our family. It is to these young people that I owe much.

Rumi is the youngest, a volatile, versatile, bubbling mass of Mathematics, pottery, arts and crafts, fashion designing, sparkling alertness, sculpting, general awareness, computers, his mobile phone, music, books and a strong sense of identity that has been shaken and traumatised, but has nonetheless held true. He is very sure of who he is and that is never to be compromised by norms and boundaries. When he was a little boy, he lay on his belly and 'did numbers' with his fat, little fingers. We created his alter ego, Canina, the Green Nail Polish Lady's daughter. Rumi never did the bad things Canina always did. Sometimes Canina did not wear her seat belt and when *Abbu* braked hard she went splat against the windshield of the car. Canina also did the unforgivable; she pulled out bookmarks from Ghazal and Azad's books! Once when he was a year and a half, Rumi decided that he would go to a party with us, but he would not wear any clothes. We were getting late and beginning to get quite desperate, so after much cajoling and pleading, and some yelling too, a pointy finger and a two-finger *pitti,* slap on his bottom, Adil belted him into his car seat, stark naked, and we drove off. All through the drive Adil told him Canina stories and what happened to her when she arrived at a party with no clothes on. By the time we reached our destination, Rumi was fully clothed and ready to be a charming guest. Through the entire party he sat on the top step of a short staircase from the kitchen to the living area, and with his chopsticks, deftly picked grilled prawns off trays coming down from the kitchen.

I suspect he is Adil's favourite, though both he and Adil would be mortified that I thought so. I have a photograph at home, of him at ten months, sitting in Ghazal's lap, and it looks like he is going to jump out of the picture, jump out of his skin! He has mapped his own life and learning, taking no advice or suggestion, self-schooling himself through high school and choosing his own college and university with no discussion. He is deliberate and fair, and a confirmed feminist. In preschool he was exposed to the Christian church. One day he came to me, excited by a discovery, and said to me, "You know what *Ammi,* god is a woman!" I figured, Mary is the mother of Jesus, and Jesus is the son of God, so God must be a woman, since there is no mention of Jesus's father. He, more than most, can learn anything, teach himself anything, be it tying the knots in macramé or untying the knots of Lie Algebra. When writing his undergraduate thesis he did both at the same time and it was fascinating to watch him tie a knot here and untie another there. Our rather plain IKEA bed got a beautiful macramé headrest and Rumi got his undergraduate degree.

I have seen the same multitasking when Rumi was in elementary school. From his Hindi homework he could effortlessly go to the kitchen and bake a gingerbread house, or was it two giraffes kissing (?), surrounded by a ring of dancing people. The paints of a social studies project would get transferred to a wooden box. The floor of his room was littered with bits of yarn, paint, glue, pieces of fabric, interspersed with school books and the clothes shed for last night's shower. He used to do his school work, especially the unpalatable parts, quickly and efficiently. Then he would luxuriate in all kinds of projects of his own making. No one could look in, not into the schoolwork nor into the more creative pursuits. We never disturbed him nor insisted on seeing what he was doing. In time he himself would share with me his creative projects, but never the schoolwork. Whenever I got the opportunity I would clean up his room, but largely we left him alone. He was a happy child, sometimes a little stubborn and demanding, but Azad and Ghazal had taught him to take no for an answer: "*Ammi* will always say no first and there is nothing you can do but wait for her to come round," and he had learnt his lesson well. He also loved to watch television. Ghazal, who had hardly been allowed to watch television at that age, tried to explain to him that worms would come out of the television set and enter his brain. This is something Ghazal firmly believed until quite old; but it had no effect on Rumi, as by then even Canina had faded into the twilight. Notwithstanding all this, his academic reports were excellent.

In the first term report of sixth grade, Rumi's teacher wrote that he had 'mood swings.' This term was the definition of a very specific psychological state and had too many negative connotations for me; I was concerned and a little annoyed, so I went and met the teacher. The teacher said Rumi did not always listen to her and did as he pleased. That sounded like stubborn to me. Was he wilful? No. Was he disruptive? No. Did he do his work? Yes, always, but he was moody. Was he sad sometimes? No, just moody. We were about to move to Sweden and I did not want Rumi to start school life there with 'mood swings' pinned to him, it just sounded so much more drastic. I had not known him to be even moody, perhaps because at home and within our family he had nothing to be moody about. Not even when I was his teacher in Sweden later on and attached to him 24 hours a day, which gave him all the reason to be moody. Maybe the sixth grade teacher saw something we didn't because we were not looking closely enough.

I am in touch with my children round-the-clock, seven days a week. Roby once wondered about that, but it is what they want too. I remain a bridge between them and many of our family and friends, and I don't intrude upon their larger world. There was the email, but then I wrote too much, some of which they did not read, and rarely ever replied to. Then the phone; that cost too much. Now there is Skype and WhatsApp, and email still for graver matters that don't need a response. Rumi can talk endlessly in a call, as he goes about washing dishes or cooking dinner or surfing the net, wanting to tell me about the shampoo he got or the four sided grater, sending me pictures of the ramen he made for dinner or the Christmas lights *Abbu* got for him in Stockholm or his septum piercing or the teapot tattoo on his wrist, wanting to talk about his friends and the pub crawl they went on. Interspersedly he talks of more serious matters too, but then I sometimes hear an edge to his voice. Ghazal and Azad are more reticent, but they do allow me to call and tell me about their part of the world, so I never feel they are behind closed doors. And they describe in some detail what they are cooking! Every single conversation ends in, "Ok *Ammi* I've got to run. I'll call you later," and I quote Mirza Ghalib to them:

> *Tere vaade par jiye hum, to ye jaan jhoot jaana,*
> *Ke khushi se mar na jaate agar aitebaar hota,*

> If I lived on your promise, this life would be a lie;
> Would I not have died of happiness, if I believed you?

With all three of them I feel it is they who are bringing me up, and not I, them. I have often told Rumi that the best way to understand Mathematics is to teach it to someone else. I think I feel the same way about parenting. I allow them to parent me, and urge Adil to do the same, so we may learn from them how to bring them up in return. It works most of the time.

Through the generations

How many roads must a man walk down
Before you call him a man?
Yes, and how many seas must a white dove sail
Before she sleeps in the sand?
Yes, and how many times must the cannonballs fly
Before they're forever banned?
The answer, my friend, is blowing in the wind
The answer is blowing in the wind

Bob Dylan

Zurich lasted for only a year. It was a diffused sort of grey year, but not so dismal and dark. When we moved there I had vaguely contemplated working in a school, but soon realised that was not going to be possible. My mind and limbs were fettered by a terrible inertia and trying to work with children was a formidable thought. I was hankering to go back to Bangalore.

Rumi was most unhappy about this. He started arguing with us, wanting to stay back at a boarding or with our friends in Leuggern. These were intense, but contained arguments, made with a certain amount of teenage angst, and we figured it was to be expected. Summer was upon us and we started looking for schools for him in Bangalore. He took little interest in this endeavour, though agreed that he should go to an international school. We took a trip to the US to visit my siblings and their families; he resisted until the very last minute, saying that if he had to move to India he should at least be allowed to spend his last summer with his friends here. Even meeting Azad and Ghazal was not an attractive thought. He remembers me saying that my family was more important than his friends, something that makes me very sad every time I think of it, because I truly believe that you, and you alone, define which relationship is important to you and which is not; it is not a given. Once there, he refused to relate to anyone and a certain moodiness set in, with bouts of angry tears. In this state we moved to Bangalore. Adil still had six months of work in Zurich, so it was Rumi and I who moved.

We could not find reasonable accommodation in town, and after two weeks in a hotel we moved into a very expensive, very ugly, poorly lit and damp serviced apartment, on a narrow street full of potholes. Every time we pass this street Rumi remarks how depressing he finds it. The only redeeming feature was that it was in the central area of Bangalore and so the school van came there. Rumi started in an international school, a long bus ride away. On the first day I went with him and sat outside until it was time to go home. This school lasted a week, as it had snooty children from rich Bangalore families and Rumi felt he had nothing in common with them. He found himself another international school, an even longer bus ride away. There he noticed that the foreigners treated him like an Indian and the Indians treated him like a foreigner, and he was caught between the two. Still, he liked the IB programme in general and some of his courses in particular, and it looked like it might work.

Rumi was still moody and angry, and this came out in sharp rejoinders in many instances. He was doing his school work, even if he was doing it at the last minute. He normally slept late, as he had done in Zurich, and did not like getting up in the morning. Each morning, when it was night for Ghazal, she would call and wake him up; he still didn't jump out of bed, but those few minutes of speaking to his sister seemed to set the tone for his day.

One evening Rumi said to me that he was ready to break his non-vegetarian fast of the last five years. He was happy and relaxed with his decision and we went to Hard Rock Cafe to have a burger. He said he had some school work, but he would do it after dinner. The burger went in slowly, contemplatively and we went home. His light was on until very late at night and then it was turned off. Ghazal could not call the next morning, so I went to wake him up with some trepidation. He didn't want to get out of bed, saying he was very tired from working last night and that he didn't want to go to school. He had just got into the cycle of school and homework, and not wanting a break in that I started to cajole him insistently; started to push him, as he saw it. In agitation he jumped out of bed and got dressed. The school van had already left, so I took him to school in a taxi and he sat through the ride in hostile silence.

I cannot describe how I felt. For some time I hung around near the school buildings, told the school administrator that Rumi was not well and I could take him home if he wanted, then sent Rumi an SMS; his reply disturbed me even more. Then I sat in the taxi 50 yards from the school gate for the rest of the day. I was still trying to extricate myself from the silent greys of Zurich and found myself torn apart by the uneasy worry for my son that was fast becoming loud sounds in my head, voices decrying my efforts. I was in a state of stunned exhaustion by the time Rumi came out. During the ride home the hostility turned to belligerence.

Rumi ran ahead of me and once we were inside the apartment, he pushed me away with a force that spoke volumes of the turmoil inside him. He ran from room to room, screaming expletives, climbed on furniture, locked himself in the bathroom; seeming to want to get away from himself, as much as from anyone or anything else. This was not teenage angst; this was not the Rumi that I knew. Something terrible was happening. I called a friend who I knew counselled young people. She took him for a ride and to have *dosa,* a savoury crepe; Rumi neither ate nor spoke. While they were gone I looked at my miserable surroundings: the seepage in the wall, the fungus hanging like stalactites from the ceiling, the dented pots and pans, and felt wronged at being charged such an exorbitant rent for this rubbish. Wearily I got up and called Adil, who was still in Zurich. I did not really know what to tell him, that Rumi got angry with me for waking him up in the morning and sending him to school? However, he was quickly able to surmise the gravity of the situation and took the next flight out to Bangalore. Then, not being able to bear the uneasiness, I called a friend and told her what had happened. In some misguided sentiment of sympathy and consideration for me, she said, "Oh, poor you. What about you, Sara? Just tell him to stop it!" My hackles rose. Here I was telling this woman how my son is suffering, and instead she was reducing him to wilfulness and me to righteous self-pity. My mind whirled. When will people learn that this could be an illness, which you cannot stop just by telling it to? Can you just cure diabetes by talking to it? Rumi is a well brought up child and what happened to him today is not a flaw in his character, nor a laxity in his self-control. I said nothing.

Rumi came home bone weary. He had not had a morsel to eat the entire day, maybe not even a drop of water to drink. After the tirade earlier he could not speak, could not cry, did not even blink. He sat in a chair with his eyes wide open and nothing was going in or coming out. When I told him his *Abbu* was going to be here soon and everything would be all right, he gave me a little smile and agreed that we should cook mushrooms with garlic and chilli for dinner. That night he held my arm with both his hands, as he struggled to sleep. I watched his face, not changed much from when he was a baby, watched his eyelids droop over eyes that were always full of life, heard his breathing become even, felt his hold loosen on my arm and knew he would sleep the night safe with his *Ammi.*

With Rumi secure in bed I got up and called Azad and Ghazal, also to tell them that Adil was already on his way. Azad, as he was wont to do in every crisis, stilled my fears and stayed my mind. I discussed the possibilities with him and he agreed that we should see a psychiatrist as soon as possible. With Ghazal it was a longer conversation. At first she kept saying, "Oh no," and was very disturbed. She felt bad that she had not called to wake Rumi up that morning; Ghazal and Rumi have a special bond, and Ghazal feels a responsibility towards him. In the 25 minutes we spoke, she had decided to talk to her professor at Rockefeller to allow her to go back to India, permanently, as her younger brother was facing difficulty. She was not making a sacrifice, she was simply delineating a priority.

A tired and still quite sleepy, but not so unhappy Rumi met Adil in the morning. With Adil there, I too felt less diffident and overwhelmed. In the early hours of the morning, before Rumi woke up, I could give him a proper account of the events of the previous day and we discussed the necessity of seeing a psychiatrist. I was not sure if Rumi would agree and the other problem was of finding a good psychiatrist, as I had not consulted a psychiatrist in Bangalore until then. I decided to find the psychiatrist first and only then broach it to Rumi.

Through the internet we found a highly acclaimed psychiatrist, so with my calmest demeanour I spoke to Rumi and asked him whether he should perhaps see a psychiatrist. With some relief he said yes, and I realised that he too was frightened by this unleashed Rumi he didn't know. As Adil was with Rumi, I collected my thoughts and wrote down an account of Rumi as I had known him for 16 years, and what I had experienced yesterday. I gave it to Rumi to read. He just glanced through it and returned it to me without a word. Armed with this piece of paper, Rumi, Adil and I went to see the psychiatrist.

We were revolted by the filth and stench that met us as we entered the hospital where the office of the psychiatrist was. Not a good start. When our turn came, I asked Rumi and Adil to remain outside, while I went in with my piece of paper to prepare the ground for Rumi. The doctor, who looked like a clone of the visa officer at the US consulate a lifetime ago, took my piece of paper and read it quite quickly. Then he asked for the patient. When Rumi came in he handed my sheet to him and asked him, "Is this true?" This time Rumi read it in detail, read every expletive, read his disturbing SMS, read all that he had done, said, and with each word his head hung in shame. He picked up his head and said, "Yes, it is all true," and in almost the same breath asked to leave. We left, never to go back.

Adil had to go back to Zurich in three days and it was imperative that we find a psychiatrist. Dr N was no more, something I did not know. I had not met him since our Delhi days, but he was always there to reach out to, to seek advice from. It was a great personal loss to me, but I was held so tightly by drugs, I could not grieve. Just like I cannot grieve or be sad about many things while they still cause me excruciating pain. We were introduced to a lady who presented herself as a good enough option. She was very interested in taking on Rumi as a patient and said she found him 'fascinating.' Adil left and we started a regimen of doctor visits. In this time Rumi went back to the school only once, to celebrate Diwali, pick up his things and say goodbye. The school wrote to us expressing concern, but I did not reply. It was official that Rumi would not attend school anymore. Adil also moved us out of the crummy cesspool, the serviced apartment, into luxurious dwellings, where they made our beds every day, like in a five star hotel, and the sun streamed in from floor to ceiling windows.

What did all this do to me? For one, it picked me out of the grey silence I was in and threw me into dark, murky noise. We were refurbishing our apartment and I was found yelling at the workers more often than I should have been, because I felt they were not doing their job. I got work in a school as a quasi-learning consultant for Mathematics, only to discover that they were not really giving me any meaningful work, not even teaching. I was working three days in the week; I would go in the morning, drink coffee during breaks, eat lunch and the rest of the time I would simply faff around, pretending to work on tasks that I made up. I still don't know why they took me on. I felt friends were sidelining me. We have a large group of friends in Bangalore, but during the six months that we were in the two serviced apartments, just two came to visit, one because Adil was visiting. Friends had heard of my Sweden breakdowns, whatever they may have made of that. They were also wary of my intense peaks during the earlier years when they were ignorant of my illness. Even from then, there was a slight cooling off, but now they gave me a wide berth. And with me; Rumi. I heard it said that I was insufferable, mean, a mercenary, rude, covetous, callous, possessive, impetuous, arrogant, immature – and much more that I do not wish to recall. Not many knew about Rumi, and from the ones who knew, hardly anyone reached out. It was the same with close friends from out of town, sometimes we did not even get to know they were visiting. What wouldn't I have given to be asked out to a seafood restaurant, where Rumi could have his spicy prawns and I, my fish curry; where we could laugh and talk of things that did not matter; as we did once. At least I think we did, but it is so very long ago, I can no longer remember.

The feeling of being wronged was like bile, which spewed out in emails, in phone conversations, in person, in unrelated events and with unrelated people, and left a bitter taste. There were major or minor eruptions continually. I left the school after putting everyone in their place, or so I thought. I screamed at a friend, long distance on the phone, for not standing by us, for rejecting us. I felt marginalised and harboured resentments that were not entirely of my own making. But the intensity of my reactions was extreme. I incessantly wrote emails to siblings, cousins and friends, incensed with dark thoughts.

Things were hotting up and something had to be done before things got more out of hand. I used to accompany Rumi to the psychiatrist once a week and asked her if she would see me as well. She was a nice person who tried to get to know Rumi and me in sessions that were each an hour long. She borrowed my copy of An Unquiet Mind by Kay Jamison. She came with me to Woodsong, when I described to her my intense hypomanic state at the time when I built it. She gave me the glad, then happy, then elated, then euphoric, and finally ecstatic, sequence of progressively more manic states; no wonder she was unprepared for us, unprepared to address the third dimension of manic depression; the hypomanic anger that Rumi and I exhibited, soon to become manic as a consequence of her intervention. In one session she allowed Rumi to unburden himself to her, while I sat outside the room, something I was not too happy about; on principle I did not leave Rumi alone with a psychiatrist. She later told me that Rumi spoke at length about his parents, his grandparents, his friends, his grouse against the school in particular and against returning to India in general. All this, she said, was causing him anxiety and making him depressed; she would have made an excellent therapist. She asked to start him on an antidepressant and an anti-anxiety pill. From my experiences I was wary of this line of treatment, in case he was bipolar, and shared my concerns with her. "Mrs Sara, just because you are bipolar it doesn't mean he is too. You have to stop seeing yourself in him." Chastised, I kept quiet and Rumi started on his medicines. In this time Adil came back from Zurich with his calm practicality and basic good sense, Ghazal came back from New York with her cycle in her checked baggage, and Azad and I discovered the potential of Skype. This certainly took a load off my shoulders.

I developed diabetes around this time. It was the psychiatrist's considered opinion that Olanzapine, the antipsychotic drug I was on, is diabetogenic, and she abruptly withdrew the drug, saying that I did not need it in any case. I did think of Dr ES and Abilify, but did not say anything. I also needed a new prescription for Lithium, as I was running out of the stock I had brought from Zurich. The Swiss Lithium was Lithium sulphate, while the Indian is Lithium carbonate, and this necessitated some molar calculations. The psychiatrist made these calculations, or so she said, and started me off on the new Lithium, all the while trying to convince me to switch to Lamotrigine, as this was a drug she was more familiar with.

Very quickly my serum lithium levels started to fall far below the therapeutic range. With the lithium stronghold reduced and the antipsychotic support no longer there, I fast became psychotic, and this found me on 11/11/11 at 11:11 am outside her office, without an appointment, asking politely, but menacingly, that I be referred to a pharmacologically more experienced psychiatrist! I wanted to say 'pharmacologically more competent,' but didn't. I had my own molar calculations for Lithium sulphate and Lithium carbonate, dug out from my Chemistry memory of 30 years ago, which were presumably different from her calculations. She was somewhat alarmed and I could sense her discomfiture. She referred me to a Dr X, so I could clarify my doubts, and he took matters into his capable hands. I think she sent me just for the serum lithium levels to be adjusted and was expecting me to come back, as Rumi was still with her; she was peeved to realise that I was not going to.

In the meantime Rumi began to yo-yo up and down on the 'happy happy' medicines, as he called them, that she had given him. He stayed up nights and sometimes round-the-clock. He would get into a frenzy of doodling, painting, eating, cursing, dancing, singing, and bouts of anger – and then descend into a void. When in deep despair, he did not want to live anymore; he was so, so tired that he wanted to go to sleep and never wake up. He would hold on to me tight and say, "Fix it *Ammi,* don't show me how, just fix it." And this would be repeated ad nauseam. He put on weight and this negative image of himself dragged him further down. Adil decided to take matters into his hands. He and I went to meet Dr X and I took my sheet of observations, now grown into several sheets. Dr X took a long time to study these sheets and then said, unequivocally, that Rumi was most clearly bipolar. Adil immediately called the other psychiatrist and told her that Rumi would no longer come to her; there could have been a kinder, less abrupt way to say this, but we were under enormous stress. We did not have the luxury to stand on any kind of formality and break it to her gently. Adil tells me she took this with very bad grace. In retrospect, it seems now that I was taking control, fiendishly rooting for a diagnosis, a specific diagnosis of bipolarity, almost willing it to be so. So many people, in addition to the psychiatrist, had said to me that I thought Rumi was bipolar because I was bipolar. But I knew he was, right from the start. I was getting desperate as I did not want him to suffer the indignities of an incorrect diagnosis; as I had.

We knew Ghazal was different, from others and from me. Sure I was able to find bits of me in her as also bits of Adil, but she was a very different person, a complex person, and we found solutions for her in time. The time lag was much more for Rumi. It took us much longer to realise that he was not as simple and straightforward as he seemed, took us more time to find solutions for him and we made many more mistakes. Consequently, he suffered much more pain. He was always somebody somewhere, even nowhere, his emotions firmly in place despite their volatility. For me, he was my mirror image, I saw in him many of my own emotions and that is where I missed the fact that he had his own sense of being, which was perhaps a nobody somewhere or even a nobody nowhere. These gaps were not in sync with mine, these gaps were not something I saw when I looked in the mirror that was he. Then he lived through my two devastating episodes in 2007. The extreme polarity of my moods was like a slow breath sucked in, polarising his emotions. I was too ravaged by these episodes to look and find a mirror in his eyes and soul. I was too impressed by his maturity at 12 to realise that this very maturity was becoming a conduit for deranged adult emotions to his very being. Very slowly, in an almost fluid motion, we watched his emotions split down the middle.

Dr X was the designated psychiatrist from that time on. Initially Rumi had difficulty opening up to him and maintained a moody silence during our visits; I would talk on his behalf. Slowly he started adding his bits, more often to contradict me and sometimes to agree. He also began to accept Dr X's rather pedantic mores. Dr X was very, very patient with him and he was very patient with Dr X. With time, a doctor-patient bond developed. Rumi still did not always go to see Dr X when he was supposed to, and I took with me detailed notes when I met the doctor on my own instead; when he did go, he still did not always talk. Five years thence, the doctor was most pleasantly surprised to find Rumi, for the first time, openly and rationally discussing this illness and its treatment with him. We found in Dr X a very compassionate man, a real gentleman, who did not pry into our affairs and yet got a sense of our family values and appreciated them.

Dr X started Rumi on a mood stabiliser, Sodium valproate, and slowly weaned him off the antidepressant. This made a significant difference. Rumi still went up and down, mostly down now, but learnt to pick himself up by doing various handicrafts with yarn – wool, rope, string, thread. It was remarkable how the feel of yarn between his fingers would still his anxieties and it was reassuring to find him start a new project after every dip. In this state he completed his high school in 2012, from home, schooling himself with the help of some wonderful adults from various walks of life. Basically he wanted to study Mathematics and English Literature. Aside from this he was ready to study any subject from the long list, as long as it allowed him to fulfil the requirements for Cambridge AICE. He mugged one of these subjects for just a week and a half and got a C. It was a reason to be proud that he completed his high school with merit, along with the rest of his peers, despite the troubled times, His high school diploma is one of the most precious and hard earned treasures that we have.

Dr X also stabilised my serum lithium levels. I took my molar calculations to him; he just smiled and asked, "You did this?" and nodded in approval. Adil had read that after a while Lithium may not provide enough stability by itself and upon his request Dr X added a very small dose of Risperidone, an antipsychotic. I have been stable on this prescription for the last five years, until recently when Dr X had to reduce my Lithium intake, as it had begun to affect my parathyroid and the accompanying blood calcium levels. This, by the way, is something I discovered from my readings on the internet. Since I had been told numerous times that I cannot believe everything I read on the net, with some trepidation I checked with my niece, who is an endocrinologist, and then brought it to the notice of my endocrinologist and Dr X. They all concurred.

Rumi took a year off after high school, a gap year I am told it is called. The first part of the year was spent in writing college applications, to the US and Europe. He would disappear into his room and shut the door firmly, only emerging to get food from the fridge. Every time I found him behind the open door of the fridge I would remember a childhood ditty, *'kya khaayen kya peeyen kya le pardes jaayen,'* what shall I eat, what shall I drink, what shall I take to a foreign land? This little bit of nonsense would lighten his mood and he would go back to his applications. The door of his room stayed firmly shut until he emerged with two or three admissions, and chose to go to Germany.

The question often raised was whether all this would not have happened to Rumi had we not moved back from Europe, as that is what started it. I put this question to Dr X. He explained to me that moving back to India was a trigger for the illness, not the cause. When this illness exists, anything can be stressful and become a trigger; so if it was not this, it would have been something else. When re-adjusting back in Europe, in Germany, Rumi was under enormous stress again and his college years were turbulent. When I shared this with a friend, she asked, "But why? He is on medication." For some reason we automatically assume that a mental illness can be 'turned off' with medication. That doesn't ring true. It is like any other illness that is treated with medication. The medication has to be finely tuned to physical health, lifestyle, environment, etc. In the first instance, this tuning process is quite difficult; then, if the doctors do get it right and then if something changes in this web, it is all out of whack again. *Apia* has hypertension, as did *Amma*. She doesn't smoke, doesn't drink, eats less salt in her food, follows all the doctor's orders and is on a regimen of diuretics and hypertension medicines, as well as many other medicines. Still her blood pressure randomly shoots up for no apparent reason. The fine-tuning can be near perfect but it cannot be 100 per cent, and it is a continuous battle.

Rumi went from crisis to crisis in Germany. In the first semester, things became so bad that he had to drop the term and come home. He went back and he persevered with the most remarkable determination. Dr X looked after him long distance, and once he had a German psychiatrist prescribe for him when he started to go down and up relentlessly. Dr X concurred with the doctor, who added the antipsychotic Risperidone to the mood stabiliser Rumi was already taking. Dr X explained to me that if a drug is effective for one member of a family then it is likely that it will work well for another member of the same family. The effectiveness of Risperidone for me was well established by then. When Rumi came home that Christmas, he explained to Dr X that the most worrisome were the lows, as he just kept going down and could not lift himself out of it. At some point he would be catapulted to a kind of hypomanic high, and then descend low again. When he was low he could not do any work, sometimes not even get out of bed; sometimes he would rapid cycle, so all this would get repeated in a short span of time. Dr X listened to him very carefully and prescribed him an antidepressant, Bupropion. So he was now on Bupropion, the antidepressant, to lift him out of his lows, Risperidone, the antipsychotic, to fight psychotic thoughts and Sodium valproate, the mood stabiliser, to try and keep him on middle ground so the antidepressant did not make him manic. This was the most optimal for a while until it was not, and Rumi went very low again. The doctor then decided to change the mood stabiliser to Lamotrigine, but the switch had to be done very slowly and the drug carefully titrated into his system. It could have terrible, initial side effects, one being that skin starts to peel off. This combination has held Rumi together for two and a half years, but is still not foolproof.

In Rumi's final undergraduate year, Adil and I moved back to Zurich. It was comforting to be close at hand and he could visit often. Sometimes he would bring a take home exam or a home assignment, and come to Zurich. We cooked, went shopping and watched Doctor Who; and made pots of tea in between. I saw how brave and strong he was, how purposefully driven, how determined, and I derived my strength from him. Once he was low about himself and I made him a list of his positive qualities – "You are stable, despite everything, honest, loyal, very intelligent, essentially happy, very brave, firmly feminist, determined, unbiased, caring, sensible and so much more that I cannot find words for." The list keeps growing as I find words to describe this amazing young adult. Now he is in Uppsala, Sweden, studying for his Master's in Mathematics. When he began there, the stress of adjusting again to a new place, to new people, destabilised him and he had a mixed manic-depressive episode, when negative thoughts and emotions gained a manic high. He was feeling wonderful, full of energy and on the go. He is always fearful that the expansive feelings of grandeur and grandiose thoughts about himself will lead to a crash thereafter. The crash came as expected, but this time it was not a simple, straightforward descent. It was accompanied by physical sensations and hallucinatory imaginings. His acute perspicacity and clear insight into himself made it possible for him to recognise what these were, so he could go and seek treatment at the psychiatric emergency of the university hospital. This was extreme mania of the negative state, and his courage in the face of it is very heartening; it is at the same time worrying, as a psychotic episode of this magnitude can totally impair judgement. His hypomania or mixed hypomania, which he had experienced until now, may have graduated to mixed mania. He was prescribed an additional antipsychotic, Quetiapine. I was reassured by his presence of mind and his courage, yet concerned by the inexorability of his illness. The psychiatrist assigned to him specialises in young adults, 18 to 25 years of age. I now see the Swedish logic in a psychiatrist seeing a patient a long while after an episode. Rumi agrees with me that the best time to see a psychiatrist is when you are well, so you can clearly describe yourself when you are not well. Rumi described himself to his doctor, verbally and on a lengthy form. He was amazed at how intrusive the questions were and how thorough the assessment. He also met another student with a similar condition, who tells him that here in Sweden there is a possibility of being one and a half bipolar. If your symptoms are more severe then you are bipolar I and if not so severe then you are bipolar II. However, if your symptoms are more severe than bipolar II but not quite as severe as bipolar I, then you may be found somewhere in between! I spoke to Dr X and he said he has come across this in psychiatric literature too. This knowledge came as an amusing relief to Rumi, who definitely does not want to live with the burden of full-blown bipolarity I. As I have done very well with Lithium for many years, his doctor tentatively suggested adding Lithium to Lamotrigine for him, but that is still under consideration.

Rumi is not cowed down by his illness and lives university life to the full, without any compromises. He does have to regularise his sleep and take his medicines on time, as insufficient sleep and gaps in medication have him spiralling down almost immediately. I have set an alarm for 20:00 and he allows me to send him a message every night, so there are no unsettling pauses in his living. Our whole family spent Christmas and New Year with him in Uppsala and he was a perfect host, seeing to all our needs, despite the fact that we crowded his little apartment all day, which quite overwhelmed him.

How am I? My pillbox has ten and a half tablets to take each day and there is an insulin injection to take every night, to battle bipolar disorder, hypothyroidism, hyperparathyroidism, high blood calcium, high cholesterol and diabetes. The Lithium dehydrates me and I drink gallons of water; you can imagine the consequence of that. My eye is developing cataract and my bones, osteopenia. But I feel well. There is some amount of short term memory loss. I forget what I am thinking, even as I am thinking it, and sometimes forget a word in the middle of a sentence, thus the urge to put things down in writing. I almost cannot read a book. My hands have developed more than a slight tremor. I can't find things; if I am looking for something in a cupboard or cabinet, I look for it at a height level where I know it should be, but to the left or the right of it, mostly the left. The children and I call it 'lateral displacement' in jest. I still blow up and have difficulty crying. In a recent meeting Dr X explained to me that psychiatrists have their antennae up for what they call 'disorder' talk versus normal talk. Even a bipolar person must sometimes get normally hurt and angry, and I do, even if its expression is somewhat different and more exaggerated. I cannot read but do write; I recognise that troubled or flying thoughts do not make for good writing, even if you are writing about them. I lie awake in the moments between the dawn and the dark of night, searching for that simple highway, that still eludes me.

My biggest loss is that people stop listening. When I get intense or angry, many say I am getting manic and turn away. I get desperate and often start to shout. When I don't shout, I use incisive language or sometimes use multiple words with just shades of difference in meaning, to get the sentiment across. I call it my 'three synonym syndrome'. The psychiatrists might perhaps call this a heightened awareness of an elevated state of mind; the uninitiated may well call it idiocy, but I do find distinct semantic differences between words that are generally deemed synonyms. I reckon it is better than shouting in capital letters!

Djinnaat Rooh

Dard-e-dil likhoon kab tak,
Jaaoon unko dikhlaa doon,
Ungliyaan figaar apni,
Khaama khoon chakaan apna

Mirza Ghalib

Until when shall I write the pain in my heart,
I should go and show them,
My wounded fingers,
The blood dripping from my pen.

Babajaan calls my spirit a *djinnat rooh,* the spirit of a *djinn.* It is demonic mental energy gone amok. I spent a couple of evenings with Ghazal's friend, associate and housemate during PhD studies. Since no one in either home was in town, we met to have dinner and take in a show for which I had free tickets. After dinner, and carried into the next evening after the work day, she and I got talking about states of mind. She has studied Neurobiology and is, therefore, familiar with the biochemical aspects of a chemical imbalance in the brain. This, however, does not automatically translate into a psychological, a clinical picture of what a bipolar disorder really means on the ground, for the person experiencing it. She wished me to describe what I knew and had experienced. I realised how hard it was to do so.

Manic-depressive bipolarity does not present itself merely as two extreme states in a two-dimensional representation. I have experienced it as a continuum of states ending sometimes in extremes in, at least, three dimensions. Extremes of what, happiness and sadness? Depression, for me, was not an extreme form of sadness, just as mania was not an extreme form of happiness, though each contained elements of its descriptor, sometimes in very exaggerated form. These contained many other elements too, sometimes mixing together so they could not be contained in these two dimensions.

A characteristically happy person is not necessarily manic, but in a manic state happiness has no real basis or boundaries; it quickly amplifies into states of elation, euphoria and ecstasy, the mind flying high on bits of disjointed, positive sensations and thoughts, as perceived by the mind. Conversely, depression is not an extreme form of sadness. Sadness is a concrete emotion rooted in reality, whereas depression is devoid of both emotion and reality. Depression is a sinking into a state of lesser emotion, lesser feeling. Depression may begin with sadness but that is only a trigger. It then sinks lower and lower and becomes a state unto itself, a pessimistic, anxious, paranoid state where there is no feeling, nothing is happening and nothing can happen. Where mania is marked by unrealistic, unlimited hope, the hallmark of depression is utter hopelessness.

I also look upon manic (or hypomanic) and depressive states as varying degrees of pure emotional energy, energy that rides on itself in a bipolar individual and does not need the substance of thought or rationale. It is this mental energy that makes the mind soar ahead when you are manic. You are special, you are connected to everything and everyone; nothing is impossible; you are beautiful and there is beauty in everything. There is no need for sleep and this energy keeps you going in a hyperactive state. The sheer force of this energy conjures up images and sounds that are not there and you have hallucinations. People walk and talk all around you and they are looking at you and communicating with you.

When this energy has not left all rational thought behind and there is some underlying truth to your expansive state, then it is a hypomanic state. You are creative and productive, still in a hyperactive, maniacal sort of way, but you don't allow the energy to get uncontrollably high or even miserably low to descend into depression. I was in sustained hypomania when I built Woodsong and I have not forgotten the incredible feeling associated with it. In Sweden, when a nurse asked me if I missed this state, I thought this an odd question. Why would I miss any part of my illness? And then I thought, this being such a persistent, acute and chronic disorder, there must be some times when I felt better than others. A sustained hypomanic state is just such a time; when your energies match your capabilities, your activity is in sync with your creativity and you are in a perfect, tense balance, even if not a stable equilibrium; and without the necessity of control. With a sense of gratitude I realise that I have been much privileged. I was able to sustain this hypomania many times in my life, besides the creation of Woodsong: when bringing up my children, which I continue to do even today, when cooking with my family, when playing the sitar, when teaching middle school in Singapore, when sewing funky appliqué quilts, when making a home in different parts of the world, when studying for BEd in Delhi and when writing.

And then there is depression, a state of low and lower, and yet lower emotional energy, to an extreme when you are devoid of any energy at all. Rumi and I have both experienced this state. Rumi more than I, has been severely depressed in the regular course of his illness. I have not been in a state of depression by itself or as a precursor to mania; my rise into mania is quick, definite, almost instantaneous. However, I have met depression in the post-manic, heavily medicated periods.

Rumi's depressions begin with a certain listlessness, a lassitude, a malaise, an overwhelming tiredness, a need to be alone behind closed doors, a rejection of people, lack of food, lack of sleep. These are interspersed with volatile bursts of anger and sometimes uncontrolled rage, as he descends lower, to a point where he is unable to lift his head from the pillow. I read the first four books of Harry Potter to him when he was seven. Years later, when I saw him like this, I used to think, "This is what the dementors do to you." Earlier, these bouts of depression would last over days and weeks, uninterrupted, but with the correct medication now, the time span is significantly reduced. The bursts of anger and crying brought relief, albeit momentary. He would calm himself down or lift himself up by 'doing Maths', as he called it, or knitting or crocheting or weaving a piece of macramé.

My depression, which I have experienced twice in its extreme form, once in full measure and the other time somewhat less, but for a longer period of time, was a direct descent into an abyss, a vortex of fire, a black hole. The dementors had sucked out my spirit and there was not even a crutch left for me to lift myself with, the first time around. For a year the first time and two to three years the second, I had no or little emotional, mental or physical energy. Sweden and beyond I had Rumi to look after and so had schooled myself in the bare minimum motions of life. Yet these were largely emotionless motions. The phrase, 'do not feel like doing anything,' falls short of describing this state, as there is no 'feeling.' As Rumi has said to me more than once, "I would rather be manic any day than be depressed." In extreme depression, the temperature of your spirit reaches absolute zero.

In later years I experienced mixed states and Rumi experienced a severe mixed state just some weeks back. These are states described as having elements of both mania and depression. A little difficult to understand in terms of energy levels since we have defined mania as made up of high and higher energy and depression as low and lower energy. Then Ghazal mentioned the possibility of a third dimension and I began to work along those lines, Rumi's illness was by then confirmed and I had one last episode as I struggled with him. This was a hypomanic episode, but totally different from the ones before. The anger, the intense feelings of being wronged, the hatred, the paranoia, were all negative emotions that would normally create conditions for anxiety and depression. But they didn't. These feelings were elevated into maniacal rage, aggression, expressions of anger, ranting emails, foul language, biting sarcasm, a sort of mental energy given to negative thoughts... There was nothing creative about it, though I do sometimes read, in a sort of morbid fascination, what I wrote in those emails, and it was entirely destructive in nature. It was in close association to reality, not just perceived reality. It was psychotic nonetheless, even though there were no hallucinations and only minor illusions, but many delusions. The short, intense, dark episode that Rumi had recently, was mixed manic born of a plunge into depression.

What doctors want for you is 'euthymia,' a balanced state, a placid, calm and harmonious state, where creativity is balanced by optimal stress, unlike the hypomanic state that is pulled by tensions. Here you are ideally active, not overactive or underactive; where you go about the business of life with a calm fortitude, where daily routine is important with seven to eight hours of sleep, where your life is at best minimally productive even if you are so bored; if you are satisfied with this and can sustain this, you are well. They would advocate a life of quiet routine: take long walks, sit on a park bench and read a book in sunlight or just nod off, do some sewing, invite people for dinner or go to someone's house in the evening, but not to high-strung parties, do housework and take a nap in the afternoon, just half an hour or 45 minutes, or you will not be able to sleep at night. Whether you are creative or not is not their concern, whether you are stimulated or not, by anything, not their problem. In fact, it is best not to be too stimulated and creative, as that carries with it the risk of dislodging this balance of energies.

It brings to mind again my *Abba's* dictum, that to be bored is good. For people like him and me, and now Rumi, who are unable to harness their emotional energies either way, it is imperative to be able to remain at the baseline, often, and not have tensions pull you up or down. The inertia that is boredom may not allow a certain kind of creativity that requires me to be in the throes of excessive mental energy, but the quiet calm it affords me is very therapeutic and can be productive. I used to hate doing house chores, finding them a waste of my time and talent; especially dusting, until one day I discovered that it was quite palatable if I wore sports socks on my hands, turned on Michael Jackson, and danced my hands on furniture and books and the large number of curios we have. Many years later a woman refused to work in our house if she had to dust with socks! I had to buy her dusting rags. Occasionally *Amma* would pull me up for the state of my house and I knew she had seen Adil washing the dishes or wiping the kitchen counter or washing a window or cleaning the bathrooms, no matter how late at night it was, because I wouldn't do it. *Amma* was all for men doing housework, she just wasn't for women not doing it. As luck would have it, I had a mother and a husband with a fetish for cleanliness and tidiness that I didn't share. Tehmina says I keep beautiful homes wherever I live, so I must have acquired some. On a more sombre note, after the many trials and tribulations that she has been through, Tehmina wrote to me, "All I can tell you is that every house you have lived in immediately became home to me. And the larger significance lies in the fact that this was so even when the house I myself lived in didn't seem at all like home." Oh heck, is all I could say.

I did the housework, nonetheless, and still do it, because I don't want Adil to do it all. But now I find it so comforting to knead dough and roll out *rotis,* find solace in the hum of the vacuum cleaner, the swish and tumble of the washing machine, the whirring in the dishwasher, the groaning and rumbling of the dryer. I can sense the feel of warm, soapy water as I wash dishes and the clean crispness of the freshly laundered sheets as I change the linen. I still don't like doing housework, but do find therapy and healing in it. When I savour the sizzling spices, as they sputter and burst open, filling the air with their fragrance, I realise that cooking is no longer such a chore. It has risen up this emotional energy ladder to become truly inspirational, as I cook alongside Adil, or one or the other of my children. We are a family of gourmets, of foodies in modern-day parlance, who incessantly talk about food, cook food and revel in the nuances of flavour as we churn out epicurean meals.

Adil says I was always a good cook but one day decided to start cooking tasteless food; so he had to cook. The children say I wouldn't cook so they started cooking. Neither is strictly true, but my cooking must have gone up and down with my mood.

Then there is the sewing, something I have always enjoyed doing in moderation. *Amma* and I started an appliqué *razai,* a quilt, for Ghazal, with her bookshelf appliquéd on it. It took very long to make it and was quite laborious, but I completed it. It was to be her tenth birthday present, but became her fifteenth. Ghazal took it to college and brought it back in shreds. I was not disappointed, as she had got good use out of it, and I saved some of the pieces. In Rumi's years in college, when he was struggling and troubled, I needed something to do, to keep myself sane. I made seven appliquéd *razais*, a graduation doll and a number of tote or sling bags, the graduation *jholas,* for my children and their friends; and a mildly pleasant activity, that could be just a chore, became a quirky art form, keeping me composed.

From Adil's aunt I learnt to stitch a *gharara,* an exquisite piece of geometry made up of rectangles and diagonals that magically unfurls into a flowing garment. Sewing it is like writing poetry. When Azad's friend, for whom I had stitched a gharara earlier, had a baby girl, I stitched her a *chatka,* shocking pink, baby gharara. That was quite a challenge as I had to make space for a nappy and keep things in proportion; but what a delight.

Strangely enough, it is this same optimal slowing down of mental energies in bland Genferstrasse 30 that affords me the calm each time I sit down to write, allowing me to look deep into my thoughts and find the words to say them. It is not possible to catch thoughts on the fly.

I can now differentiate three distinct states, actually four if you count euthymia. There is the manic state which rises on the positive scale of mental and emotional energies. Life moves fast, thoughts are rapid and singularly positive, happy and grand, and words trip over themselves. When still rooted in reality, but an exaggerated form of it, it is a hypomanic state. Depression brings with it a slowing down of life and thought, sinking below the euthymic level. This is a debilitating state, a low-energy state, a negative state on the scale of mental and emotional energies, and is peculiarly devoid of words as a means of communication. Distinct from these two states is the mixed state. It is a state which is negative in its emotional, mental content, it comprises negative thinking, but instead of pulling you down as in depression, it elevates these very negative emotions in a third dimension of the emotional energy scale. It puts you in a hypomania or mania that has turned dark. When hypomanic in this state, there is deluded anger, aggression, and vituperative and abusive words come hard and fast to express these feelings. Rumi's recent state bypassed this hypomanic state and included paranoid hallucinations and dark physical sensations, to manifest itself as a mixed manic state.

I can visualise these four distinct states and their juxtaposition very clearly. I do not, however, have the mathematical or computer skills to make us a three-dimensional, graphical representation of them, as Ghazal has suggested. Perhaps one day Rumi will.

The sense of 'self'

Khudi ko kar buland itna, ke har taqdeer se pehle
Khuda bande se khud poochhe, bata teri raza kya hai

Allama Iqbal

Take your 'self' to such heights that before every decree of fate
God himself asks you, tell – what is your consent?

There were no mirrors in Mishkat, except for *Abba's* shaving mirror and a tall mirror I had inherited from *Apia* in 7 Shibli Road, which must have broken before I came of age, as I don't remember using it. In Woodsong, as in other houses we have lived in around the world, there were only bathroom mirrors set above the washbasin. Rumi wanted a mirror so Ghazal could see for herself the wonderful creations he made for her, and we got him a tallboy with a mirror attached on one side. This was wedged between his bed and his bookshelf, so Ghazal had to squeeze against the bookshelf awkwardly, on Rumi's insistence, and admire the ensembles he created for her; no one else could get to it. I, therefore, only rarely glanced upon the ravages of my illness. I was grateful for this, especially in Mishkat, where I never got to actually see the amorphous mass I had become.

Now I think of Zehra Nigah's *sher:*

Din raat ki gardishien musalsal,
Shaanon pe thahar gayi hain saari,
Chehre ka pighal raha hai sona,
Baalon pe baras rahi hai chandi

and know that

The constantly revolving day and night,
Have all come to settle upon my shoulders,
The gold is melting away from my countenance,
Silver showering on my hair.

Even now I don't look closely in the mirror, but do look at my reflection in the eyes and faces of people who love me, and still find myself beautiful.

My self-esteem took a beating, again and again, crushing my spirit, so I had no regard left for myself, perhaps no sense of self. The pain was excruciating at times and exquisite at others, but it was pain, metaphysical pain, born of turmoil and anguish. I now believe what I have been told all along, but never quite understood, that this turmoil and anguish are really a part of me, an intrinsic imbalance in my brain, and are not demons to be exorcised. Nor are they actually caused by outside factors. Just some of life's situations use this unbalanced mind as a schema, a platform, for them to act upon and shatter my sanity. I am beginning to believe this imbalance may well be chemical in nature; at least chemicals, in the form of drugs, bring considerable relief, whereas talking and psychotherapy do not.

There are many, many writings that I have not included here; they serve no purpose except to showcase the deep gashes in my soul. Yes, this is an illness, a physical/chemical disorder, but its symptoms have psychological, social, ethical ramifications. Unlike diabetes, where the mind knows that you have diabetes and so prevents you from having sugar, here the mind itself is impaired; in the event of an episode the mind may not even be aware that emotions are peaking. The world around you may or may not know that you have bipolar disorder. Those who are told, read up on the internet and come to believe that you are sometimes happy and sometimes sad, and discover that you are quite intolerable the rest of the time. How bad could that be? It takes unconditional love and a lot of courage for people to envision the rest: the pain of anxiety and paranoia, the delusions of grandeur that get shattered, the haunting hallucinations that you cannot differentiate from reality, the complete loss of control over mental faculties, the raging anger, the overpowering urge to obliterate yourself – and above all, to realise that these psychological symptoms are just that, the symptoms of an underlying physical, neurochemical balance gone wrong. These are not wilful acts. I have no control over my actions, whether in mania or depression, or at any other time; they are not really me. But then the question arises, am I just a bunch of chemical reactions, some of which are the norm and so acceptable, the others that step away from the norm and make me different, special in Adil and the children's eyes, insufferable in some others'. The thought used to bother me, but it doesn't anymore. If this is true for me then it is true for everyone else. I'd rather be me.

The most difficult thing for me was to deal with people and relationships; I wanted all or none. With the best of intentions, people could not really understand this bizarre thing that was happening to me. Although no one ever really turned away, they did back away, they did avert their eyes a little, they stopped being proud of me, they began to find excuses for me and to stand on emotional formality with me. To be truly empathetic needs a lot of dauntlessness and a lot of effort. I know so many who have this moral courage and are willing and able to make this effort; there will always be some who are unable to. As Adil said to me, everyone has problems; who knows what problems of their own they have to contend with.

As the pain became more and more unbearable, I started to perform a lobotomy on my thoughts and feelings, not to forget them or set them aside, just to cut them clean out of my psyche. I never sat and mulled over things that did not work out, like my Master's at IIT Kanpur, another Master's in the US, the PhD in the US, the teaching job in Bangalore, my failed relations with people close to me, my abortive attempts at research and teaching. I could not afford to dwell on these, as the accompanying loss of self-esteem was immeasurable. So I developed the faculty to say, "No, I do not want any of this," and mean it. The more I wanted something, the more devastated I was by its loss, the more rejected I felt by others, all the more vehement would be the negation, until the thing ceased to exist as far as I was concerned and I was momentarily at peace again. *Amma's* advocacy: "There is no reason to dwell upon something you cannot change." When Mishkat was felled, I had, for so long, ridden over the pain of losing it, it did not hurt at all. When *Babajaan* told me our house near Zakaria Market had been demolished, I couldn't breathe for just a split second, something squeezed at my heart for a moment and then the feeling was gone; it was totally gone.

And, I learnt to count my blessings.

The agony and the ecstasy remain, to this day, to torment me or exalt me, but my sense of who I am is firmly established and preserved; almost.

I have never, unequivocally, answered Stephen Fry's question, posed in his documentaries, The Secret Life of the Manic-Depressive: If you had the choice, would you still choose to have bipolar disorder? Or, as he phrased it, "If you could press a button to release yourself from bipolarity, would you?" There is no straight 'yes' or 'no' answer to this question. Yes, I would choose to have bipolar disorder because that is what I have and it makes me who I am. Also, I am more than the sum total of my illness. In 2003 I cut my knee-length hair and the fashionable bob gave me an identity crisis. When I came home from the hairdresser's, Azad went all shy when he saw me and said, "Oh hullo *Ammi,"* as though meeting me for the first time. It took me 14 years to grow my hair and be able to pull it back into a bun, making me 'myself' again. I would have a far worse identity crisis if my emotions were chopped off. There is, of course, the pain and trauma associated with extremes of mood and emotion that I can live without. Yes, I would press the button, but only halfway, and it would have to be a pretty sophisticated piece of equipment that releases me from the irrational, psychotic mania, the dark despair of depression and the negative, destructive emotions of a mixed state, but leaves me with glorious hypomania and the contentment and rest of euthymia. May I be forgiven for audaciously soliciting the best of both worlds, but if it can't do all this, then I will not press the button.

~

Oh, I'm bein' followed by a moonshadow, moonshadow, moonshadow
Leapin and hoppin' on a moonshadow, moonshadow, moonshadow

And if I ever lose my hands, lose my plough, lose my land,
Oh if I ever lose my hands, Oh if... I won't have to work no more.
And if I ever lose my eyes, if my colours all run dry,
Yes if I ever lose my eyes, Oh if... I won't have to cry no more.

And if I ever lose my legs, I won't moan, and I won't beg,
Yes if I ever lose my legs, Oh if... I won't have to walk no more.
And if I ever lose my mouth, all my teeth, north and south,
Yes if I ever lose my mouth, Oh if... I won't have to talk...

Cat Stevens

~

And this, as Adil would laconically say, is the psychlinis of my life.

A prayer to *nigaar-e-hasti*

Aaiye haath uthaein hum bhi,
Hum jinhein rasme dua yaad nahin;
Hum jinhein soz-e-muhabbat ke siva,
Koi but koi khuda yaad nahi.

Come, let us also raise our hands (in prayer)
We who do not remember the custom of prayer;
We who, except for the burning fire of love,
Do not remember any idol, any god.

Come let us make a petition
That beloved life
Would pour the sweetness of tomorrow (future)
Into the poison of today (present).

For those who have not the endurance
To bear the heavy burden of the passing day,
May it lighten night and day
On their eyelashes.

For those whose eyes do not have the courage
To face the dawn,
May it light some candle
In their nights.

For those whose steps have not even
Support of a path,
To their sight may there be
A way apparent.

To those whose religion is advocacy
Of lying and hypocrisy,
May they get the courage to deny,
The audacity to seek the truth.

To those whose heads are awaiting
The sword of oppression,
May they have the ability to shake off
The hands that slay.

The mysterious secret of love is
The fevered soul, with which
Let us make an agreement today
So the fever be gone.

The word of truth pricks the heart
Like a thorn,
Let us express it today so
The troubling sensation be gone.

Translated from *Dua* by Faiz Ahmed Faiz

www.ingramcontent.com/pod-product-compliance
Lightning Source LLC
Chambersburg PA
CBHW051252250726

48656CB00004B/1253